Instructor's Manual and Test Items
to accompany

Intercultural Communication

Everett M. Rogers
Thomas M. Steinfatt

prepared by

Diane M. Millette
Thomas M. Steinfatt
Eva Hericks

University of Miami

WAVELAND
PRESS, INC.

Prospect Heights, Illinois

For information about this book, write or call:
Waveland Press, Inc.
P.O. Box 400
Prospect Heights, Illinois 60070
(847) 634-0081
www.waveland.com

CONTENTS

Introduction 1

Part I: Sample Course Syllabus 3

Part II: Chapter Objectives, Outlines, and Case Illustrations 11

Chapter 1: Context and Contact 13

Chapter 2: The Study of Intercultural Communication 16

Chapter 3: Culture 19

Chapter 4: Communication 23

Chapter 5: Verbal Communication 28

Chapter 6: Nonverbal Communication 31

Chapter 7: Assimilation, Mass Communication, and Sojourning 34

Chapter 8: Becoming More Intercultural 38

Chapter 9: The Global Village 42

Part III: Discussion Topics and Activities 45

Part IV: Test Items (Multiple Choice, True/False, Essay Questions) 69

Chapter 1: Context and Contact 71

Chapter 2: The Study of Intercultural Communication 78

Chapter 3: Culture 84

Chapter 4: Communication 91

Chapter 5: Verbal Communication 97

Chapter 6: Nonverbal Communication 104

Chapter 7: Assimilation, Mass Communication, and Sojourning 110

Chapter 8: Becoming More Intercultural 116

Chapter 9: The Global Village 122

Introduction

The instructor's manual for *Intercultural Communication* is divided into four parts:

- Part I provides an overview of the course including sample syllabus, course outline, and assignments.

- Part II provides learning objectives, extended outlines, and case illustrations for each chapter.

- Part III provides various discussion topics and activities.

- Part IV includes examination questions for multiple choice, true/false, and essay items.

Intercultural Communication, by Rogers and Steinfatt, examines the exchange of information between people who are culturally unalike. The essence of intercultural communication is the way in which different cultural values, beliefs, rituals, behaviors, artifacts, experiences, and worldviews—the sets of variables which form the differences between cultures—affect the ways in which people process information. This book discusses how people from different cultures come to see things differently, and how those perceptual differences affect their communication. These communication effects occur (a) in the processing of messages, such that quite different meanings are created from those of persons in another culture; (b) in the selection of messages to encode others; and (c) in the nonverbal behaviors that accompany and modify verbal messages, including situation and communication environments.

PART I

Sample Course Syllabus

University of Miami
CCS 545: Intercultural Communication (IC)

Fall, 1999
Tuesday, 6:25 to 9:05pm
Section UX, MB113A

Professor: *Dr. Thomas M. Steinfatt*
Office: Merrick 113; E-mail: tms@miami.edu
Phone: 284-2265 (School); 284-3354 (Office)
Office Hours: Monday & Wednesday 12:00 to 4:00pm; and by appointment
Home Page: http://www.miami.edu/com

Required Textbook: Rogers, E. M. & Steinfatt, T. M. (1999). *Intercultural communication.* Prospect Heights, IL: Waveland.

Recommended Textbooks: Hall, E. T. (1959). *The silent language.* Garden City, NY: Doubleday. Ting-Toomey, S. & Korzenny, F. (Eds.) (1989). *International and intercultural communication annual XIII: Language, communication, & culture.* Beverly Hills: Sage.

Prerequisites: CCS110 (Communication Theory) or graduate standing or permission of instructor.

Course Description and Objectives: To provide you with information and experiences that will help you:
(a) To understand the reciprocal effects of intercultural perceptions on policy, and of policy on intercultural perceptions, in the history of Eastern-Western relations;
(b) To understand the way communication functions in intercultural settings;
(c) To understand how culture affects the communication process; and
(d) To understand the role of historical, political, and religious factors in creating cultural stereotypes, perceptions, fears, desires, and misunderstandings.

5

Areas of Emphasis: CCS545 concentrates on Western interactions with non-Western cultures. It examines:
(1) Religion, cultural factors, the history of interaction with outside ideas, and attribution processes in intercultural communication;
(2) The history of intercultural interactions between the East and the West;
(3) Cultural assumptions in Western/non-Western communication interactions; and
(4) Linguistic relativity and other language factors in intercultural communication.

Course Requirements and Evaluation

- Attendance (see policy)
- Required readings (see schedule)
- In-class experiences and lectures
- Presentation (Graduate & Honors Students)
- Exam 1   40%
- Exam 2   30%
- Ethics Paper   10%
- Term Paper   20%
                              100%

Attendance Policy: Attendance is required for this course. Since this class meets only once each week, you are allowed ONE absence during the term, excused or unexcused. If you are absent more than once without formal excuse, your grade will be lowered. Excuses must be presented within a week of the day you return from the excused absence or the absence will count as unexcused. If total absences go beyond two, regardless of reason, the instructor will attempt to accommodate the student, but such accommodation is not guaranteed, and repetition of the entire course is a likely outcome.

Examinations: Examinations will contain both objective and essay items. The first examination will cover all readings, assignments, and class material up to that exam. The second examination will cover the material since the first exam. There will be no comprehensive final exam in this course. Several objective questions on each exam will cover questions asked in class concerning matters of geography and knowledge of important intercultural events or persons. For example, "Who, what, and where is *Diego Garcia* and what is its intercultural importance?" "Who, what, and where is the world's largest religious structure and what is its intercultural importance?"

Ethical Position Paper: One of the principle problems encountered in intercultural interactions concerns policy decisions, either personal, corporate, or national: When should a person, an organization, or a state intervene in the affairs of another person, culture, or state? How do we tell the difference between customs that simply offend us versus acts that are unethical and that we have a moral duty to act against? What is the difference between an unethical act, implying a universal judgment based on an ethical system that applies to all human beings, versus one that is merely tasteless and perhaps lower class, as judged by the standards of the person making the judgment and as embedded in that person's culture?

A brief typed paper is due at the third class meeting (Tuesday, September 14) in which you are to state your own ethical position in four pages or less. The paper is your attempt to deal with the questions raised in the previous paragraph, and it must answer the question: "How do you know when an action is right and when it is wrong in an intercultural setting?" How does such an action differ from one that is merely not in accord with cultural norms? Be exceptionally clear about this distinction in your paper. Use at least two examples of actions that would be considered "right" by one culture and "wrong" by another culture, stating the difference in concept of right and wrong in these cultures and how your position would handle those problems. Feel free to use (or not use) the ethical system of a particular religion (e.g., the Ten Commandments of Judaism and Christianity), but defend your position, what ever it is. Demonstrate your knowledge of North American culture versus other cultures in the paper. Your paper will not be graded on the ethical position you choose to defend. It will be graded on your defense of your position and your discussion of the right/wrong examples. Does your position hold across cultures, or is it culture bound, and how much thought have you put into your position as intercultural? You do not need to cite sources nor to include a reference list. By the end of the class, you should be able to examine your personal ethical position as presented in your paper and state what, if anything, you would want to change and why.

Term Paper: Select any topic or any area of intercultural communication that interests you. Write an eight page (undergraduates) or 12 page (honors students and graduate students) paper on the topic. Use the *Publication Manual of the American Psychological Association (APA,* 1995) reference format. Graduate students and honors students will present their work to the class during one of the last two class meetings. Feel free to consult with the instructor prior to selecting a topic. You will be graded on following *APA* style as well as on content.

- You have an automatic extension of the paper due date to 6:30pm on Tuesday, November 30, without penalty.
- NO further extensions will be granted.
- All graduate and honors students are to be ready to present by November 23.
- Graduate and honors students are to prepare a one- to two-page handout that outlines and summarizes their presentation to the class.
- It is your responsibility to keep a copy of all papers and materials turned in for credit. (Never turn in the only copy of any paper to any instructor.)

Honor Code: The *University of Miami Honor Code* will be in effect.

Course Schedule*

WEEK	DATE	TOPIC	READINGS
1	August 31	Course Introduction Definition of Intercultural Communication (IC)	Chapter 1
2	September 7	Ethics in IC	Chapter 2
3	September 14	Attribution Theory in IC *Are the Gods Crazy?* DUE: Ethical Position Paper	
4	September 21	The Effect of Religion on Cultural Interactions, Current and Historical	Chapter 3 Handout: Religion
5	September 28	A Levels-of-Meaning Model of Communication	
6	October 5	A History of Eastern/Western Interactions	Chapter 4
7	October 12	History and Policy in Eastern/Western Interactions	Chapter 5
8	October 19	Linguistic Relativity	Handout: Linguistic Relativity
9	October 26	Review	
10	November 2	EXAM 1 (Chapters 1–5, handouts, class lecture & discussion) Nonverbal Factors	Chapter 6 Handouts: The Shower, Space & Traffic

11	November 9	The Language of Poverty	Chapter 7
12	November 16	Becoming More Interpersonal	Chapter 8
13	November 23	The Communication of Innovations Introducing Change to Other Cultures & Societies DUE: Term Paper	Chapter 9
14	November 30	Review Graduate & Honors Students Presentations	
15	December 14	EXAM 2 (Chapters 6–9, handouts, class lecture & discussion)	

* Any changes in the *Course Schedule* will be announced in class.

"Culture hides much more than it reveals, and strangely enough, what it hides, it hides most effectively from its own participants."
—*Edward T. Hall*

PART II

Chapter Objectives,
Outlines, and Case Illustrations

Chapter 1: Context and Contact (pp. 1–38)

In chapter 1, we begin the study of intercultural communication from the perspective of history. An understanding of the relationship of history to intercultural communication is important to the student's ultimate grasp of the lessons of intercultural communication.

Chapter Objectives:

For each of the following concepts and topics, the student should be able to:

(a) define the concept or topic
(b) explain its importance for intercultural communication
(c) explain the differences between similar or related topics

Concept/Topic	Page
Why Study Intercultural Communication?	2
Collective Cultural Consciousness	3
Increasing Intercultural Contact	4
The Spread of Islam	7
The Crusades	8
Genghis Khan and the Mongols	12
Ogadai Khan	14
Kublai Khan	17
Marco Polo	19
Colonialism	21
The Slave Trade	23
The Early Missionaries	28
The Opium Wars	29
Native Americans	31

The historical context of chapter 1:

(a) Shows what happens in human interaction when *respect for other cultures* is not held as a value.
(b) Holds true today as well as in past times.

(c) Great historical events often become the stuff of myths, partially true and partially embellished, which form the *collective cultural consciousness* of a nation or society.

(a) The great historical clashes during the spread of Islam, the Crusades, the attacks of the Mongols, Western imperialism and colonialization, the African Slave Trade, and the annihilation of Native American civilizations, to name but a few, can be understood in part as representing what happens to humanity when cultural respect is lacking. These lessons are not just lessons of the past. Whenever we see a lack of respect for different cultures, we see the beginnings of an attack on the disrespected cultures. Disrespect for cultural differences need not occur across national boundaries, as between Europe and the Mongols.

(b) Disrespect for cultural differences can occur across religious boundaries as in Northern Ireland between Catholics and Protestants, or in Palestine, between Muslims and Jews. It can occur across lifestyles, between straights and gays. It can occur across skin color boundaries, as between blacks and whites. It can occur between potential immigrants and current residents, as in Cuban immigration in Miami. It can occur between age groups. It can occur between persons with and without disabilities. It can occur across groups varying in physical attractiveness.

These are only a few examples of clashes that illustrate the various levels and aspects of lack of respect and its consequences. We might say that those who do not study history, and do not understand why it has occurred as it has, are doomed to repeat it. It is through the study of history and the consequences of failure to respect other cultures that intercultural communication is provided with a way of approaching the concept of respect in intercultural relationships.

(c) While individual members of society usually have not experienced the semi-mythical/semi-historical events for the culture as a whole, the events become part of its defining elements. If there is one thing we are not in the West, it is barbarians. We cherish the notions of an ideal civilized society, even if we are not always able to live up to those ideals. Thus, in the West, Genghis Khan is the reviled unwashed barbarian who eats raw meat and drinks the blood of animals. He is the destroyer of civilizations, the unfeeling murderer of kittens, babies, and little children. The Christian West defeated the barbarians, and threw them back to the East from whence they came, thus defending religion, culture, and country, (or so much of the West believes, though that is not what happened). In modern day Mongolia, Genghis Khan is the greatest of heroes, the founder of the nation and of civilization itself, an equally mythical interpretation. All cultural groups use historical figures and historical events as part of a story called collective cultural consciousness. This collective consciousness, this shared, often unspoken and unrecognized, view of reality, is then used to motivate the members of the culture to action, and to explain and rationalize the actions of the culture and its members. The role of the 16th century Battle of Kosovo, where the 16th century Christian Serbs threw back the Muslim advance into that part of Europe, in the Serb explanation of their motivations and actions during the 1999 war is one example.

Is there a world collective consciousness? Pierre Lvy, a professor at the University of Paris who teaches media studies, suggests that the Internet is creating a world collective consciousness. Students interested in the concept of collective cultural consciousness on a worldwide level may wish to read more about this notion in *The Chronicle of Higher Education* of July 13, 1999, also available at http://chronicle.com/free/99/07/99071301t.htm.

Case Illustration:

The *Case Illustration of Cortes and Montezuma* (p. 22) discusses one of the most famous cultural misunderstandings between Europeans and the original peoples of North America.

Chapter 2: The Study of Intercultural Communication (pp. 39–77)

Just as chapter 1 presents a brief history of intercultural contact, in order to set the stage for the study of intercultural communication, so chapter 2 covers a history of the study of intercultural communication.

Chapter Objectives:

For each of the following concepts and topics, the student should be able to:

(a) define the concept or topic
(b) explain its importance for intercultural communication
(c) explain the differences between similar or related topics

Concept/Topic	Page
The Roots of Intercultural Communication	39
What Is a Stranger?	40
The Stranger and Scientific Objectivity	43
The Concept of Social Distance	44
The Concept of Marginal Man	45
The Concept of Heterophily	45
Cosmopoliteness	46
Critical Concepts in Intercultural Communication	47
Ingroups and Outgroups	49
Ethnocentrism	50
Cultural Relativism	55
Prejudice and Discrimination	55
Stereotypes	58
The Authoritarian Personality	58
Intercultural Communication after World War II	59
Development Assistance	60
The Ugly American	61
The Foreign Service Institute	62
Edward Hall, Founder	63
Time Talks and Space Speaks	67
Forming a Paradigm of Intercultural Communication	70
Non-Western Perspectives on Intercultural Communication	74

Pages 39–59 discuss the origin of many of the concepts used in the study of intercultural communication, such as:

- *The Stranger:* An individual who is different from oneself culturally.

- *Social Distance:* The degree to which an individual perceives a lack of intimacy with individuals who are different in ethnicity, religion, occupation, or other characteristics.

- *Marginal Man:* An individual who lives in two different worlds, in both of which the individual is a stranger.

- *Heterophily:* The degree to which two or more individuals who communicate are unalike.

- *Cosmopoliteness:* The degree to which an individual has a relatively high degree of communication outside of the individual's local system.

- *Ingroups and Outgroups:* A collectivity of people with whom an individual does (ingroup) or does not (outgroup) identify.

- *Ethnocentrism:* The degree to which other cultures are judged as inferior to one's own culture.

- *Cultural Relativism:* The degree to which an individual judges another culture by its context (as opposed to ethnocentrism, which judges others by the standards of one's own culture).

- *Prejudice:* An unfounded attitude toward an outgroup based on a comparison with one's ingroup.

- *Discrimination:* Overt behavior that treats individuals unequally on the basis of their race, gender, or other characteristics.

- *Stereotypes:* A generalization about some group of people that oversimplifies their culture.

- *Authoritarian Personality:* A set of related personality factors relating to prejudice and discrimination. The authoritarian personality wishes to give orders and have them obeyed unquestioningly. But the authoritarian also wishes to receive orders from someone else and to obey these orders without questioning them, thereby attempting to remove ethical responsibility for actions by the removal of choice.

Pages 59–77 discuss the bringing together of these concepts by Edward Hall into the beginnings of the formal study of intercultural communication at the Foreign Service Institute after World War II. Hall's early work, some of which was published in 1959 as *The Silent Language*, formed a Western paradigm of intercultural communication.

As with chapter 1, no brief history can present all points of view, and the instructor may wish to supplement both chapter 1 and chapter 2 with additional historical examples of both historical events that became part of the collective consciousness of a given culture, or additional history of the field of intercultural communication. The role of faculty members in the Department of Communication at Michigan State University in the 1960s, such as Hydeya Kumata, and faculty in the Department of Communication of the University of Minnesota in the 1970s, such as Wilbur S. Howell (see pp. 72–74), might well be discussed by instructors familiar with those contributions.

Case Illustration:

The Left-Handed Ingroup (p. 49) discusses left-handedness as a unifying cultural feature.

Chapter 3: Culture (pp. 79–112)

The concept of culture is, quite naturally, central to the study of intercultural communication. This chapter defines a culture in terms of the beliefs, attitudes, and values held by its members.

Chapter Objectives:

For each of the following concepts and topics, the student should be able to:

(a) define the concept or topic
(b) explain its importance for intercultural communication
(c) explain the differences between similar or related topics

Concept/Topic	Page
What Is Culture?	79
Beliefs, Attitudes, and Values	81
Cultural Beliefs	82
Cultural Values and Cultural Attitudes	84
Norms	85
Collectivistic versus Individualistic Cultures	86
The Nature of the Self	89
Independence versus Interdependence at the Individual Level	90
High-Context versus Low-Context Cultures	90
High/Low-Context Communication Problems	92
Are You High-Context or Low-Context?	95
Within versus Between Cultural Variation	95
Cultural Clash	96
Cultural Identification	97
Cultural Markers	100
Language and Cultural Identification	102
Cultural Differences	103
The Continuum of Intercultural Differences	105
Overcoming Cultural Difference	107

Chapter 3 covers many of the major concepts used to distinguish among cultures. Each of these concepts concerns a dimension of cultural differences. They include:

- *Beliefs, Attitudes, and Values:* An attitude is an *emotional* response to objects, ideas, and people, while beliefs are an individual's *cognitive* representations of the outside world. Values are what the people who share a culture regard strongly as good or bad.

- *Norms:* The established, accepted, and expected behavior patterns for the members of a social system.

- *Collectivistic Cultures:* Those where the collectivity's goals are valued over those of the individual.

- *Individualistic Cultures:* Those where the individual's goals are valued over those of the collectivity.

- *High-context Culture:* One in which the meanings of a communication message are found in the situation and in the relationship of the communicators or are internalized in the individual's beliefs, values, and norms.

- *Low-context Cultures:* One in which the meanings of a communication message are stated clearly and explicitly, without depending on the context of the communication situation.

- *Within-Cultural Variation:* Variations in beliefs, attitudes, behaviors, styles, rituals, etc., which occur within one culture.

- *Between-Cultural Variation:* Variations in beliefs, attitudes, behaviors, styles, rituals, etc., which occur between two or more cultures. While between-cultural variation is usually emphasized in intercultural communication, large variations also occur within a given culture due to differences in socioeconomic standing, religious beliefs, etc.

- *Cultural Clash:* The conflict that occurs between two or more cultures when they disagree about a certain value.

- *Cultural Identification:* The degree to which an individual considers himself/herself to be a representative of a particular culture.

- *Language and Cultural Identification:* Language is often used as a cultural identifier, and many aspects of culture are often based on a common nationality or language.

- *Cultural Markers:* Any feature of an individual, such as a name, a language spoken, a way of dressing, etc., that serves as an indicator, correctly or incorrectly, of membership in a cultural group.

Case Illustrations:

Several case illustrations are presented, such as the case of *Hmong Spirits versus Western Medicine* (p. 82). This case can be controversial. Some see it as advocating an antirationalist position: "Why should we support mythical beliefs in other cultures since we don't support them in Western culture?" Others see the case as an excellent example of cultural adaptation and accommodation, where the "scientific" beliefs of one culture meld with the "traditional" beliefs of another to produce a desirable result for all concerned.

Another controversial case is that of *Female Genital Mutilation in the United States* (p. 98). This case provides the opportunity to discuss the concepts of diversity and tolerance on the one hand, versus ethical judgments on the other. Should we be completely open to all cultural practices? Would that include cultural practices such as the persecution of minorities and women? But if we are going to make cross-cultural ethical judgments, on what basis do we make them? Does a Western Christian perspective answer all problems? What is a "Western Christian perspective"? Would it justify the type of wholesale slaughter brought about by Genghis Khan in the name of a "pax Mongolia"? Many other cultures believe that that is exactly what the United States and NATO are trying to do. What do the students think, and how do their thoughts relate to their conceptions of the world, as related to their collective cultural consciousness?

An alternate tack in explaining the concepts is to ask about cruelty to animals. While most Western people react strongly to such cruelty, what is the specific ethical basis for this revulsion? Is it ethical or is it cultural? Exactly how do we tell the difference? In some Western cultures, for example Mexico and Spain, taunting a bull while slowly stabbing it to death with swords is considered great fun. Yet if a person eats at McDonalds, that person is personally responsible for the deaths of many animals in slaughterhouses. When are we justified in invoking the concepts of Western morality in other cultures? What are the rules?

Additional case illustrations in chapter 3 include: *AIDS Prevention in San Francisco* (p. 99), which discusses the diversity of approaches to AIDS prevention, recognizing the importance of very specific cultural identification in health communication implied by that diversity; *The Homeless and PEN in Santa Monica* (p. 104), discussing the effect of the Internet on a widening gap between the haves and have-nots, and one attempt to reduce this gap; and, *The Cultural Shareability of Elvis Presley* (p. 109).

Chapter 4: Communication (pp. 113–134)

The concept of communication is, not surprisingly, also central to the study of intercultural communication. This chapter defines communication as the process through which participants create and share information with one another as they move toward reaching a mutual understanding.

Chapter Objectives:

For each of the following concepts and topics, the student should be able to:

(a) define the concept or topic
(b) explain its importance for intercultural communication
(c) explain the differences between similar or related topics

Concept/Topic	Page
What Is Communication?	113
A Model of Communication	114
Initial Contact and Uncertainty among Strangers	120
Uncertainty and Information	120
Initiating Conversation with a Stranger	122
Intrapersonal and Interpersonal Communication	125
Signs and Symbols	126
Language	126
Creating Meanings	128
Levels of Meaning	129
Attribution	131
Power	133

Chapter 4 covers many of the concepts of communication itself, a process through which participants create and share information with one another as they move toward reaching a mutual understanding.

There are many possible models of the communication process. One of these is illustrated on page 115. It emphasizes the perceptions of the participants in the process, which are based in the culture of each participant. Perceptions of persons from the same culture often differ radically. When the persons are from different cultures the clash of perceptions is usually magnified.

Other important concepts covered in chapter 4 include:

- *Uncertainty and Information:* Uncertainty is an individual's inability to predict or to understand some situation due to a lack of information about alternatives. Information is anything that reduces uncertainty in a situation where a choice exists among a set of alternatives.

- *Intrapersonal and Interpersonal Communication:* Intrapersonal communication is information exchange that occurs inside of one person. Interpersonal communication involves the face-to-face exchange of information between two or more people. Communication is fundamentally intrapersonal, since internal communication and the recognition and assignment of meaning within a person are both logically and chronologically prior to the possibility of interpersonal communication. This does not mean that one is more important than the other, only that interpersonal communication requires intrapersonal communication. Yet without interpersonal communication, intrapersonal communication would develop quite differently within the individual.

- *Signs and Symbols: Signs* represent their referents directly, without the need for definition. Thus, the actual sound of glass breaking represents an actual instance of glass breaking. No human agreement on what the sound of glass breaking is to mean is needed. When glass breaks it makes a sound. *Symbols* are different from signs in the nature of the connection between them and their referent. Symbols represent their referents only through human agreement that they will do so. Thus, the use of the sounds in the words "the sound of glass breaking" is a symbolic representation of an actual instance of glass breaking. The sounds of the words represent the breaking of the glass, but they have no direct physical connection to the breaking of the glass.

- *Language:* A language is a code, a classification used by individuals to categorize their experiences and to communicate them to others. Symbols are the elements of any code.

- *Meanings Are in People:* The phrase "Meanings are in people" is a key to the understanding of human communication. It means that meanings are only in people, and nowhere else. Thus, they cannot be transmitted. For if they could, then we would not need communication. Mental telepathy and ESP would do the job for us, and we could and would read minds. People create their meanings out of the cultural nexus of which they are a part.

- *Levels of Meaning:* This refers to different levels of analysis of meaning in human communication. Communication is physical, in that a physical message must pass across physical space in physical time for it to occur. Yet its effects are in the phenomenology of the individual. While we can study the meaning people assign to words (#1), or to sentences (#2), the social meanings of importance to interpersonal and intercultural communication occur in levels #3, #4, and #5 (p. 130). These are the levels where (#3) we try to guess the other's intent in speaking to us, and in saying what is said in exactly the way in which it is said. And then we create (#4) possible scenarios based on this judgment of intent. The scenarios thus created provide the basis for our (#5) generalized views of ourselves, of other people in general, and of the world in general. The characteristic manner of assignment of intent, of creation of scenarios based on judgments of intent, and the generalized pictures of self, others, and the world so obtained, both depend upon and create culture.

- *Attribution:* Used here, attribution refers to the attribution of intent. We tend to be much more generous when interpreting our own intent than with the intent of others and see ourselves and our culture as exhibiting the normal reaction to an external event. Thus, "I" act in response to external circumstances. But we tend to believe that other people, and other cultures, act because of a hidden internal mechanism that makes them behave that way.

Thus, "You" act because that's the kind of person you are. And, people from "my culture" act as they do in response to real external events. But people from "your culture" act as they do because that is just the way people from your culture are.

- *Power:* Resources can be valued and sought by different individuals and groups. Power is the degree to which one party controls resources valued by another party. The effects of power in intercultural interactions is ever-present and often overlooked. The North American businessperson buying pineapple from an Asian street vender differs from the vender not only in culture but also in money, status, social class, and especially power. Differences between people that are ascribed to "cultural variation" usually are composed of a strong helping of differences in money, status, social class, and power, all mixed together with cultural differences.

Case Illustrations:

The case of the *Navajo Code-Talkers* (p. 117) is an excellent example of the effects of cultural diversity on success in an organizational enterprise. It also illustrates the fundamental interchangeability of standardized meanings between languages.

Don't You Want to Go to the Rat? (p. 124) illustrates the levels of complexity, which can be involved in intercultural communication. Different assumptions about language, and about cultural politeness norms, mix together with human desires and attempts to communicate to create a nexus in which humans create meaning.

The Rosetta Stone (p. 127) illustrates the importance of the differences between signs and symbols. The hieroglyphs are symbols, thus requiring agreement between humans as to what they will mean. Without knowledge of the code system (the agreements about what will mean what in a language) the Rosetta Stone was "meaningless." Once knowledge of the agreement system was obtained, the symbolic language could be understood. Signs can be understood without the need for prior human agreement. Experience with the world teaches us what signs mean.

From Intercultural Interaction to International Incident (p. 132) illustrates the effects of attributions of intent on intercultural interaction.

Chapter 5: Verbal Communication (pp. 135–159)

Verbal communication concerns language and its effects in intercultural interactions.

Chapter Objectives:

For each of the following concepts and topics, the student should be able to:

(a) define the concept or topic
(b) explain its importance for intercultural communication
(c) explain the differences between similar or related topics

Concept/Topic	Page
Linguistic Relativity	135
Examples of the Whorfian Hypothesis	138
Importance of Language	141
Perceptions Count	144
Perceptions versus Objective Reality	145
African-American and White Adolescent Girls	145
Symbolic Interaction	148
Code-Switching	148
Cultural Factors in Interpersonal Communication	149
Talk and Silence	150
Speaking Style	151
Turn-Taking	152
Self-Disclosure	152
Content versus Relationship	153
Face	154
Listening	157

Linguistic Relativity concerns the relationship of language to thought. Does the language we speak influence our thought, our thought patterns, or possibly even the logic of thought itself?

In chapter 4, the case of the *Navajo Code-Talkers* (p. 117) illustrates the fundamental interchangeability of some standardized meanings between languages. The concept of linguistic relativity suggests that such interchangeability may not always be possible. Class discussion on the extent of translatability of meaning between languages, and between cultures, is often lively and profitable. For an extensive review, see Steinfatt, T. M. (1989). Linguistic relativity: Toward a broader view. In S. Ting-Toomey and F. Korzenny (Eds.), *International and Intercultural Communication Annual XIII: Language, Communication and Culture.* Beverly Hills: Sage Publications, 35–75.

- *Perceptions Count* and *Perceptions versus Objective Reality* suggest that since people necessarily operate on the basis of the way they perceive the world to be, and not necessarily on the basis of the way it "actually is" in some metaphysical sense, perceptions are exceptionally important in communication. This is the basis for symbolic interaction. Symbolic interactionism is the theory that individuals act toward objects on the basis of meanings and perceptions that are formed through communication with others.

- *Code-Switching* is the process through which two or more individuals change from speaking one language to another during a conversation.

- Particularly important *cultural factors in interpersonal communication* are the cultural expectations concerning who will speak, when, for how long, about what, and in what manner. These include expectations about the use of silence in the talk sequence, the speaking style, and turn-taking.

- *Self-disclosure* is the degree to which an individual reveals personal information about himself/herself to another person.

- In addition to the content of a message is its relationship aspect, which refers to the *metacommunication* of the people involved, which tells them when to interpret statements as serious, ironic, funny, etc.

- *Face* is the public self-image that an individual wants to present in a particular social context.

Case Illustrations:

The Language Police in Quebec (p. 142) illustrates the importance accorded to language in society.

Perceptions of Body Weight by African-American and White Adolescent Girls (p. 145) illustrates the cultural differences in values and perceptions within the United States.

The Guest Who Came to Dinner, in Japan (p. 155) illustrates cultural differences in values and perceptions outside of the United States.

Chapter 6: Nonverbal Communication (pp. 161–188)

Nonverbal communication is communication beyond the exchange of words and verbal symbols. The meaning of nonverbal behaviors often differs across cultural contexts.

Chapter Objectives:

For each of the following concepts and topics, the student should be able to:

(a) define the concept or topic
(b) explain its importance for intercultural communication
(c) explain the differences between similar or related topics

Concept/Topic	Page
Importance of Nonverbal Communication	162
The Evolution of Nonverbal Communication	167
Charles Darwin	168
Edward Hall at the FSI	170
Raymond Birdwhistell	170
Cultural Factors in Nonverbal Communication	171
Types of Nonverbal Communication	172
Body Movements	172
Space	176
Time	181
Touch	182
Voice	184
Artifacts	184
Physical Appearance	185
The Truth about Lying	186
Cultural Misunderstandings in Nonverbal Communication	186

- *Importance of Nonverbal Communication:* Nonverbal Communication

  1. Is everywhere.
  2. Comes before verbal communication in interpersonal interactions.

3. Is very likely to be trusted.
4. Can lead to misunderstandings more easily than verbal communication.
5. Is especially important in intercultural communication.

- *The Evolution of Nonverbal Communication:* The modern study of nonverbal communication began with Charles Darwin's publication of *The Expression of Emotion in Man and Animals* in 1872. Edward Hall and Ray Birdwhistell were two of the major early contributors.

- *Types of Nonverbal Communication:* body movements, space, time, touch, voice, artifacts, and physical appearance.

- *The Truth about Lying:* Since our nonverbal behaviors are more difficult to control than what we say, considerable research on lying has focused on nonverbal behavior. There are no absolute nonverbal cues that indicate lying. But combinations of the following are related to lying:

1. More speech errors.
2. Less smiling and more fake smiling.
3. More speech hesitations.
4. Shorter answers, often yes or no.
5. Vague answers, with less specific or concrete information.
6. More slips of the tongue.
7. More allness words like "always" and "never."
8. More blinking and pupil dilation.
9. Longer pauses.

When several of these nine indicators occur together, the probability of lying increases. Paul Ekman found that people talk slightly more softly when they are lying, swallow more often, and drink water more often if it is available.

- *Cultural Misunderstandings in Nonverbal Communication:* These occur often since the appropriate and inappropriate nonverbals of other cultures are neither taught nor understood at the level and depth of understanding as are the language differences.

Case Illustration:

The Meaning of Feet in Intercultural Negotiation (p. 165). The bottom of one's foot is the dirtiest part of the body according to many Asian cultures. Displaying the bottom of the foot to another person (picture p. 167) is an insult. What do Western students see as the dirtiest part of the body? What would they think if that part were displayed to them? This question will help them to understand the meaning of feet in intercultural communication.

Chapter 7: Assimilation, Mass Communication, and Sojourning (pp. 189–220)

Assimilation is the degree to which an individual relinquishes an original culture for another. Mass communication affects assimilation by providing a sharable cultural reality through the media. Sojourning occurs when a person visits another culture for a period of time but retains the person's original culture.

Chapter Objectives:

For each of the following concepts and topics, the student should be able to:

(a) define the concept or topic
(b) explain its importance for intercultural communication
(c) explain the differences between similar or related topics

Concept/Topic	Page
Assimilation and Acculturation	190
Early Research on Mass Communication and Culture	190
The Continuum from Assimilation to Cultural Maintenance	191
Changing Demographics	194
Ethnic Groups in the United States	196
The Role of Language in Cultural Maintenance	199
Networks in the Assimilation Process	201
Contemporary Migration to America	202
The Policy Issue of Immigration	204
The Role of the Media	207
Bias in the Media	208
Impacts of the Mass Media	210
The Sojourner	211
Culture Shock	212
The U-Curve of Cultural Adjustment	214
Reentry	217

- *Acculturation* is the process through which an individual is socialized into a new culture while retaining many elements of a previous culture.

- *Assimilation* is the degree to which an individual relinquishes an original culture for another.

- The *Continuum from Assimilation to Cultural Maintenance* occurs as ethnic minorities become more integrated into the general society.

- The changes in *Ethnic Groups in the United States* during 1985–2000 have been dramatic, as illustrated by the changes in the United States workforce, from 47% Anglo male in 1985, to only 32% in 2000. The non-Anglo workforce increased from 17% to 33% of the total during that time period.

- *Role of Language in Cultural Maintenance:* Language is the single most important factor in cultural maintenance. To destroy a language is to destroy a culture. To maintain a language is central to the maintenance of the culture.

- *Networks in the Assimilation Process* refers to the tendency of new immigrants to maintain friendship networks with other new immigrants. These affiliations change over time to more associations with persons from the new culture.

- *Contemporary Migration to America:* We are currently in the greatest period of migration to the United States in its history, eclipsing in sheer numbers of immigrants the previous high period from 1890 to 1920.

- *Policy Issue of Immigration:* Most periods of large-scale immigration into any society have been followed by antiforeign backlash, with attempts to place strict limits placed on immigration. The solution to the world's problems is not to ship its population to the United States. Yet humanitarian concerns make it difficult to deny admission to people on an individual case basis. What should be the immigration policy of the United States? Should it be different for ethnic groups, which have effective Washington lobbies? How do ethnic minorities view those minority groups who get special treatment from the United States government on immigration? Is the game of "beach tag" (tag the beach and you can stay, but if we can catch you in the water you go back to Cuba), created for Cuban immigrants by current United States immigration policy, a wise and just system? If not, what would students suggest should replace it?

- *Intercultural Bias in the Media* occurs in part due to the limited ethnic representation on media staffs. When the media do not have a workforce that reflects the audience that they seek to serve, news coverage is unbalanced and ethnic groups in the audience tune out. African Americans are seriously underrepresented on United States television shows. During the summer of 1999, the adventure television series *Amazon* featured an all-white group of plane crash survivors among white natives on a continent with very large numbers of Hispanics, blacks, and Indians. Twenty-six new network television shows were scheduled for United States television for the Fall of 1999. None of them (zero) had a Black, Hispanic, or Asian actor in a lead role.

- The *Sojourner* is an individual who visits another culture for a period of time but who retains his or her original culture. Large numbers of Americans visit foreign countries, mainly for business, in military service, and as tourists. An even larger number of foreign visitors, over 12 million per year, come to the United States.

- *Culture shock* is the traumatic experience that an individual may encounter when entering a different culture. It occurs when people spend considerable energy, time, and resources to go abroad and then are not prepared for the cultural differences, which they invariably encounter. The initial euphoria over the trip turns into depression, and the person in culture shock derogates the new culture. Several cycles of decreasing levels of euphoria and depression are often experienced while abroad. Upon reentry into the culture of origin, the sojourner may experience an equally deep depression upon leaving the new culture. The original culture is now perceived as less perfect, and the limitations of the original culture stand out in sharp relief.

Case Illustrations:

Maintaining a Distinctive Culture: The Gypsies (p. 193). Gypsies have been permanent sojourners throughout history, always moving through, rather than to, another culture. They have been the object of scorn and prejudice for hundreds of years.

Ethnic Media in New York City (p. 195). The diversity of ethnic media in New York City is among the greatest of any city in the world.

You Gotta Have Wa (p. 217). *Wa* is harmony in Japan, created by what often appears to Westerners to be a series of endless and somewhat pointless meetings. How might Western decision making and organizational enthusiasm, or lack of it, appear to Japanese visitors to the United States?

Chapter 8: Becoming More Intercultural (pp. 221–241)

This chapter provides guidelines for the individual who wishes to become more interculturally competent.

Chapter Objectives:

For each of the following concepts and topics, the student should be able to:

(a) define the concept or topic
(b) explain its importance for intercultural communication
(c) explain the differences between similar or related topics

Concept/Topic	Page
Intercultural Competence	221
Overcoming Ethnocentrism	223
Experiential Training	224
Cultural Relativism	225
From Ethnocentrism to Ethnorelativism	226
Overcoming Stereotypes	227
Derivation of Stereotypes	227
Stereotypes as Codes	228
Overcoming Prejudice and Discrimination	230
Prejudice	230
Discrimination	231
Overcoming Conflict	237
Toward Multiculturalism	238

- *Intercultural Communication Competence* is the degree to which an individual is able to exchange information effectively and appropriately with individuals who belong to a different culture. Some contacts with other cultures are positive, while others are negative. Simply increasing the level of contact with another culture is no guarantee of increased intercultural communication competence, sensitivity, or tolerance. The opposite result can occur quite easily.

- *Methods of Overcoming Ethnocentrism* include positive contact with members of the other culture with perceived positive outcomes and experiential training in intercultural sensitivity.

- *Cultural Relativism* is the degree to which an individual judges another culture by and within its own context. This is the opposite of ethnocentrism, which judges others by the standards of one's own culture.

- From *Ethnocentrism to Ethnorelativism:* Ethnorelativism is another term for cultural relativism. A series of six stages marks the progression to Ethnorelativism (Bennett, 1986 [see p. 272 for full citation]):

  1. A parochial denial of cultural differences, in which there is little contact with unalike others.

  2. An evaluative defense against understanding cultural differences, because they may be threatening to one's view of the world.

  3. A minimization of cultural differences, through which cultural similarities are stressed.

  4. The acceptance of cultural differences, which are acknowledged and understood.

  5. The adaptation of one's thinking and behavior to cultural differences.

  6. The integration of cultural differences into one's own worldview, so that one's identity is both a part of and apart from the different culture, and a new "third culture" perspective replaces the native culture perspective.

- *Pluralism* is the degree to which an individual is open to others' points of view.

- *Overcoming Stereotypes:* In order for individuals to become more interculturally conscious, they must learn to question stereotypes and to break through the arbitrary borders that have been taught to separate people from one another. Rather than exerting the mental effort to evaluate all incoming information carefully and critically, we often resort to categorizing certain information into familiar patterns. Stereotypes are one of these patterns, and they can be positive or negative.

- *Overcoming Prejudice and Discrimination:* Prejudice is an unfounded attitude toward an outgroup based on a comparison with one's ingroup. Discrimination is overt behavior that treats individuals unequally on the basis of their race, gender, or other characteristics.

- *Toward Multiculturalism:* Multiculturalism is the recognition that several different cultures can exist in the same environment and benefit each other. Brazilian society and its relative acceptance of skin color based cultural differences provides an interesting contrast with the United States. How can an individual become more multicultural?

    1. Communicate with culturally heterophilous others. Seek friends who are culturally different from yourself. Travel. Learn languages other than your native tongue as a means of better understanding cultures in which these languages are spoken.

    2. Work at understanding people unlike yourself. Reading about their culture may be helpful, but you also can learn by getting to know members of another culture on a personal basis. Go out of your way to develop close relationships with unalike others. Participate in intercultural and diversity training courses that help you become less ethnocentric and more understanding of unalike others.

    3. Empathize with heterophilous others so that you can look at the world from their point of view. Be pluralistic and culturally relativistic. Do not think of ingroups and outgroups, but instead perceive of a continuum of cultural differences, such as

40

on the basis of individualism/collectivism or other dimensions.

4. Capitalize on the natural curiosity that we all have in learning about other people who are different from us. Encourage your friends and family members to become multicultural. Set an appropriate example for them to follow.

5. Understand yourself, particularly your degree of ethnocentrism, prejudice, and stereotyping versus cultural relativism, tolerance, and understanding.

6. Recognize and appreciate the cultural differences among people in your environment.

7. Be nonjudgmental of others and their cultural values.

Case Illustration:

A Navajo Perspective on Prejudice (p. 232). This case presents the experience of a Navajo woman who views her ethnic group as living under third world conditions in America.

Chapter 9: The Global Village (pp. 243–264)

The world of today is progressing toward the concept of a global village, where all of the world's people are linked together via global trade and global media into a village where every action affects others in the village.

Chapter Objectives:

For each of the following concepts and topics, the student should be able to:

(a) define the concept or topic
(b) explain its importance for intercultural communication
(c) explain the differences between similar or related topics

Concept/Topic	Page
Development Programs in Third World Countries	243
What Is Development?	244
What Is Development Communication?	244
Change Agent/Client Heterophily	246
Sustainability of Development Programs	248
Empowerment	249
Mass Media and Development	253
The Ethics of Changing Someone Else's Culture	254
Rise of the Megacity	255
The Global Business Village of Today	258
Toward a Global Culture	263

- *Development* is a widely participatory process of social change in a society intended to bring about both social and economic advancement for the majority of people through their gaining greater control over their environment. *Development communication* is the exchange of information between two or more individuals in which one individual, a change agent, seeks to assist the other individual to achieve a higher socioeconomic status.
- A *change agent* is an individual whose job is to influence clients to adopt innovations.

- *Heterophily* is the degree to which two or more individuals who communicate are unalike. *Homophily* is the degree to which two or more individuals who communicate are similar.

- The *Sustainability of Development Programs* has been very limited due to the failure to consider cultural differences during the diffusion of innovations.

- *Empowerment* is the degree to which individuals perceive that they control a situation. Increased empowerment may improve the sustainability of development programs. People tend to take pride in and take care of things that they personally "own."

- *Mass Media and Development:* Radio is particularly important as a mass medium in developing countries. The use of radio in fighting disease has been effective through the use of the entertainment-education strategy, a process of purposely creating a media message to both entertain and educate, in order to change audience members' behavior.

- The *Ethics of Changing Someone Else's Culture* provides the grounds for an important class discussion of ethics. When is purposeful change of another culture justified? Are all attempts to improve the socioeconomic status of economically developing peoples justified? Are arguments against economic development, which destroys traditional cultures, simply arguments to keep them poor?

- *Rise of the Megacity:* Megacities are cities with a population of ten million or greater. The huge increase in the world population, which will occur over the next twenty years, will occur mainly in the sprawling suburbs of the megacities of the developing world. These cities even today lack a sufficient infrastructure of roads, water supply, sewers, and electricity. Disease and resentment by the have-nots create the potential for major problems in the world of the not too distant future.

- *Toward a Global Culture:* Despite their great cultural differences, Japan and the United States have become economic trading partners and share an economic view of the future of the world. Those shared experiences, however, are far removed from the experiences in third world rural villages where much of the world's population still lives, struggling to coax an adequate harvest from a small plot of land, with traditional tools. Nor is life in the megacities exempt from deprivation, squalor and misery. How can these rural and urban poor find a voice so that their needs can be heard?

Case Illustrations:

Introducing Water-Boiling in a Peruvian Village (p. 247). Why do attempts to diffuse innovations fail? A change agent fails to consider the local culture in attempts to teach germ theory as a cause of disease.

Thrown Out on the Edge of Asia (p. 251) provides a realistic perspective on what often happens during attempts at development communication.

Los Angeles as a Cultural Mosaic (p. 257). Los Angeles International Airport provides an example of the tremendous diversity within Los Angeles.

Nemawashi: Digging around the Roots (p. 259). In collectivistic cultures such as Japan, agreement is highly prized. Just as one would not suddenly uproot a plant for transplanting without first digging carefully around the roots (*nemawashi*), one would not implement a decision in Japan without first achieving consensus among all concerned.

Gift-Giving around the World (p. 261). Gift giving in other cultures usually has strong cultural norms which provide meanings to the process often not considered by outsiders.

- *Glossary* is available on pp. 265–269.
- *References* are available on pp. 271–283.
- *Author Index* is available on pp. 285–288.
- *Subject Index* is available on pp. 289–292.

PART III

Discussion Topics and Activities

Cultural Identity Paper

Objective: This assignment focuses on two areas:

1. Individual cultural identity; and

2. Diversity of cultural backgrounds present among students in the class.

Goal: There is only one goal of this assignment—students should describe their personal cultural background. They might want to begin by addressing the following question:

What do you think is important for others to know about you in relationship to your cultural characteristics?

- Your cultural description might include elements of ethnicity, race, subculture, and/or family traditions.
- What term do you use when referencing your cultural identity?
- What misconceptions are there about your cultural orientation?
- How do you clarify these misconceptions?
- Describe specific aspects of your culture relating to the categories of *Cultural Universals*.

Evaluation: Evaluation of this assignment will be based on the depth and breath of the students' cultural description and clarity of writing. Students do not need to limit themselves to addressing only the above items. These suggestions are provided as examples of what might be included in their cultural identity discussion. Citing formal references is not necessary in this paper. Assignments must be typed, double spaced. Proof papers for grammar, punctuation, and spelling.

Cultural Deconstruction Exercise

Instructions: Ask students, as a group, to brainstorm U.S. values related to work, personal relationships, the community, etc. After the group has come up with a list, ask them to vote for the ones they consider to be most important to and/or most representative of U.S. culture. This list will serve as a basis for discussion of topics related to the film, *To Kill a Mockingbird*, which reflects U.S. culture.

Before showing *To Kill a Mockingbird*, to the class, frame the viewing of the film in the context of using its content to explain certain elements of U.S. culture to a person from another country. Give the students a list of questions (on the following page) about the film designed to serve as a guide for their viewing. As the students watch the film, ask them to identify the parts of the film that a person unfamiliar with the United States and its culture might find confusing or about which he or she would have questions. Tell them that after the film, they will use these elements to explain U.S. culture to someone who has been in the United States for a very short period of time.

After viewing the film, divide the class into pairs or groups. Ask one or two people in each group to assume the role of a foreigner in the United States and the other person to assume the role of a friend who is a U.S. citizen. The foreigner(s) should ask the American(s) about those elements of the film that he or she does not understand. The American(s) will try to explain how these relate to U.S. beliefs, history, family relationships, and the legal system, not just to the plot of the movie. Instruct each pair or group to list the questions and answers they discuss.

Ask individual students to describe some of the elements of U.S. culture, which they identified in their discussions. List these and ask the group to add other aspects of U.S. culture, which they did not observe in the film. Did they discover anything new about U.S. culture that they were unaware of before?

continued

Questions:

1. Why did segregation exist? Who were its supporters and its opponents?
2. How often did (does) black and white violence occur? Did (does) it go both ways?
3. Why did Atticus, a white man, defend a black man in the segregated south? What typically American cultural belief(s) underlay his actions?
4. Who should have been punished: Tom Robinson, the rape victim, the father, or Atticus?
5. Why did the lynch mob leave the jail?
6. Describe the nature of the relationship between U.S. parents and their children?
7. Do you think that Scout is a typical American girl?
8. How should Boo Radley have been cared for after his parents' death? Why do you think Boo Radley was allowed to live as a hermit after his parents' death? What does this convey about U.S. citizens' relationships with their government?
9. Are people in small towns in the United States typically unfriendly toward strangers? Toward blacks?

Source: Adapted from Seely, H. N. (ed.) (1996). *Experiential activities for intercultural learning*. Yarmouth, ME: Intercultural.

Cultural Universals

Below is a list of some cultural traits that are common in all cultures. Engage students in a discussion about how different cultures use the universals.

1. age grading
2. athletic sports
3. bodily adornment
4. calendar
5. cleanliness training
6. community organization
7. cooking
8. cooperative labor
9. cosmology
10. courtship
11. dancing
12. decorative art
13. divination
14. division of labor
15. dream interpretation
16. education
17. eschatology
18. ethics
19. ethnobotany
20. etiquette
21. faith healing
22. family
23. feasting
24. fire making
25. folklore
26. food taboos
27. funeral
28. games
29. gestures
30. gift giving
31. government
32. greetings
33. hair styles
34. hospitality
35. housing
36. hygiene
37. incest taboos
38. inheritance rules
39. joking
40. kin groups
41. language
42. kinship nomenclature
43. law
44. luck, superstitions
45. magic
46. marriage
47. mealtimes
48. medicine
49. modesty concerning natural functions
50. mourning
51. music
52. mythology
53. numeral
54. obstetrics
55. penal sanctions
56. personal names
57. population policy
58. postnatal care
59. pregnancy usages
60. property rates
61. propitiation of supernatural beings
62. puberty
63. religious ritual
64. residence rules
65. sexual restrictions
66. soul concepts
67. status differentiation
68. surgery
69. tool making
70. trade
71. visiting
72. weaning
73. weather control

Source: Murdock, George P. (1945). The common denominator of cultures (pp. 123–142. In Linton (ed.) *The science of man in world crisis*, pp. 123-142. New York: Columbia University

Rokeach's Instrumental and Terminal Values

Instrumental Values

Ambitious (hard working, aspiring)

Broad-minded (open-minded)

Capable (competent, effective)

Cheerful (lighthearted, joyful)

Clean (neat, tidy)

Courageous (standing up for your beliefs)

Forgiving (willing to pardon others)

Helpful (working for welfare of others)

Honest (sincere, truthful)

Imaginative (daring, creative)

Independent (self-reliant, self-sufficient)

Intellectual (intelligent, reflective)

Logical (consistent, rational)

Loving (affectionate, tender)

Obedient (dutiful, respectful)

Polite (courteous, well mannered)

Responsible (dependable, reliable)

Self-controlled (restrained, self-disciplined)

Terminal Values

A comfortable life (a prosperous life)

An exciting life (a stimulating, active life)

A sense of accomplishment (lasting contribution)

A world at peace (free from war and conflict)

A world of beauty (beauty of nature and the arts)

Equality (brotherhood, equal opportunity for all)

Family security (taking care of loved ones)

Freedom (independence, free choice)

Happiness (contentedness)

Inner harmony (freedom from inner conflict)

Mature love (sexual and spiritual intimacy)

National security (protection from attack)

Pleasure (an enjoyable, leisurely life)

Salvation (saved, eternal life)

Self-respect (self-esteem)

Social recognition (respect, admiration)

True friendship (close companionship)

Wisdom (mature understanding of life)

Source: Rokeach, M. (1973). *The nature of human values.* NY: Free Press. Rokeach, M. (1979). Value theory and communication research: Review and commentary. In Dan Nimmo (ed.), *Communication Yearbook 3*, pp. 7–28. New Brunswick, NY: Transaction.

Value Statements

Instructions: Ask students to indicate the top ten statements that they believe are the most important.

1. It is the person who stands alone who excites our admiration.

2. The individualist is the person who is most likely to discover the best road to a new future.

3. In most groups it is better to choose somebody to take charge and run things, and then hold that individual responsible, even if he/she does some things the members do not like.

4. The most rewarding object of study anyone can find is her own inner life.

5. There should be equality for everyone—because we are all human beings.

6. Good group members should accept criticisms of their points of view without argument, in order to preserve a harmonious group.

7. Not to attain happiness, but to be worthy of it, is the purpose of our existence.

8. A person's future depends primarily upon what that person does, not upon what that person feels or thinks.

9. A person has achieved success who has lived well, laughed often, and loved much.

10. A well-raised child is one who does not have to be told twice to do something.

11. The facts on crime and sexual immorality show that we will have to crack down harder on young people if we are going to save our moral standards.

12. There has been too much talk and not enough real action in doing away with racial discrimination.

13. Heaven and hell are products of human imagination and do not actually exist.

14. Let us eat, drink, and be merry, for tomorrow we may die.

continued

15. A rich life requires constant activity, the use of muscles, and openness to adventure.

16. A teenager should be allowed to decide most things for him/herself.

17. Character and honesty will tell in the long run that most people get pretty much what they deserve.

18. The most important function of modern leaders to bring about the accomplishment of practical goals.

19. In life an individual should "go it alone," assuring individual privacy, having much individual time, and attempting to control his/her own life.

20. Human nature being what it is, there will always be war and conflict.

21. Friendship should only go so far in working relationships.

22. What youth needs most is strict discipline, determination, and the will to work and fight for family and country.

23. There should be a hierarchy in an organization, with definite duties for everybody.

24. No time is better spent than that devoted to thinking about the ultimate purpose of life.

25. Depressions are like occasional headaches and stomach aches; it is natural for even the healthiest person to have them once in a while.

26. In any group, it is more important to keep a friendly atmosphere than to be efficient.

27. A person must make his/her own decisions, uninfluenced by the opinions of others.

28. Obedience and respect for authority are the most important virtues children should learn.

29. In choosing a husband, a woman will do well to put ambition at the top of her list of desirable qualities.

30. In a small group there should be no real leaders—everybody should have an equal say.

31. To lay down your life for a friend—this is the summit of a good life.

32. You have to have respect for authority and when you stop respecting authority your situation is not worth much.

continued

33. Humans should control their bodily senses, emotions, feelings, and wishes.

34. When a person has a problem or worry, it is best for that person not to think about it, but to keep busy with more cheerful things.

35. We are all born to love—it is the principle of existence and its only true end.

36. When we live in the proper way—stay in harmony with the forces of nature and keep all that we have in good condition, then all will go along well in the world.

37. A good group is democratic—the members should talk things over and decide unanimously what should be done.

38. Every person should have complete faith in some supernatural power whose decisions he/she obeys without question.

39. The past is dead, there are new worlds to conquer, the world belongs to the future.

40. The most important qualities of a real person are determination and driving ambition.

41. The greatest satisfaction in life is a feeling of the actuality of the present, of tireless activity, movement, and doing.

42. No matter what the circumstances, one should never arbitrarily tell people what they have to do.

43. The most important aim of churches should be to encourage spiritual worship and a sense of communion with the highest.

Source: Rokeach, M. (1973). *The nature of human values.* NY: Free Press. Rokeach, M. (1979). Value theory and communication research: Review and commentary. In Dan Nimmo (ed.), *Communication Yearbook 3*, pp. 7–28. New Brunswick, NY: Transaction.

Stereotypes and Attributions

Instructions: This activity asks students to identify the stereotypes and attributions that we hold about others and how these stereotypes and attributions may interfere with effective communication. Ask students to individually (and anonymously) write down characteristics that they feel best describe each of the following groups of people: Euroamericans, African Americans, Latinos, Asian Americans, Native Americans, Middle Eastern Americans, and females and males. Collect each set of descriptions and for the next class prepare an overall list of all students' responses. Distribute and read them aloud. Follow up with these questions:

1. Where did you get these descriptions? How do you know what you think you know about these groups?

2. Do you think these descriptions are generally accurate? Why or why not?

3. Why do we form stereotypes? When do we use stereotypes? Are they fair?

4. How could some of these stereotypes interfere with successful communication?

5. How can these stereotypes help in your efforts to communicate successfully with members of those groups?

6. Were you ever treated like a stereotype yourself? How did that make you feel? How did you feel about the other person?

Source: Shepard, C. A., Kearney, P., Plax, T. G., & DeFleur (1998). *Instructor's resource manual to accompany Fundamentals of Human Communication.* Mountain View, CA: Mayfield.

Self Disclosure: Public and Private Self

Instructions: Ask students to mark the following topics as either *private* or *public*.
Private: If it is comfortable to discuss only with myself, family, or intimate friends.
Public: If it is comfortable to discuss with casual friends, acquaintances, or strangers.

	Private	Public
Attitudes and Opinions		
1. What I think and feel about my religion; my personal religious views.	☐	☐
2. My views on religion.	☐	☐
3. My views on racial integration.	☐	☐
4. My views on sexual morality.	☐	☐
5. The things I regard as desirable for a person to be.	☐	☐
Tastes and Interests		
1. My favorite foods; my food dislikes.	☐	☐
2. My likes and dislikes in music.	☐	☐
3. My favorite reading matter.	☐	☐
4. The kinds of movies and TV programs I like best.	☐	☐
5. The kind of party or social gathering I like best; the kind that bores me.	☐	☐
Work or Studies		
1. What I feel are my shortcomings that prevent me from getting ahead.	☐	☐
2. What I feel are my special strong points for work.	☐	☐
3. My goals and ambitions in my work.	☐	☐
4. How I feel about my career; whether I am satisfied with it.	☐	☐
5. How I really feel about the people I work for or with.	☐	☐
Money		
1. How much money I make at work.	☐	☐
2. Whether or not I owe money; if so how much.	☐	☐

continued

3. My total financial worth.   □   □

4. My most pressing need for money right now.   □   □

5. How I budget my money.   □   □

Personality

1. Aspects of my personality I dislike.   □   □

2. What feelings I have trouble expressing or controlling.   □   □

3. Facts of my present sex life.   □   □

4. Things I feel ashamed or guilty about.   □   □

5. Things that make me feel proud.   □   □

Body

1. My feelings about my face.   □   □

2. How I wished I looked.   □   □

3. My feelings about parts of my body.   □   □

4. My past illnesses and treatment.   □   □

5. Feelings about my sexual adequacy.   □   □

Family

1. Inquiries about the health of family members.   □   □

2. Descriptions of family disagreements.   □   □

3. Problems of siblings, parents, or children.   □   □

4. The family's financial situation.   □   □

5. Social activities of the family.   □   □

Source: Adapted from Barnland, D. (1975). *Public and private self in Japan and the United States: Communication styles of two cultures*. Yarmouth, ME: Intercultural.

Cultural Effects on Communication

Instructions: Students work in groups. Assign each student one of the worldviews below. Each person must communicate as if he/she held an assigned view:

1. You believe that there is no higher power above humans. There is no spiritual realm. Truth is scientifically-documentable. Though science has validated some evidence for spiritual beliefs, it has not proven a higher power. We live one life. When we die, we cease to exist. There is no supreme justice.

2. You believe in a higher power and in a spiritual existence. Only the highest power can know all of the truth. We live one life on earth and a different, spiritual life after death. We pay for our life mistakes, after death.

3. You believe in a higher power and in a spiritual existence. Humans also contain this power and live many lives. Different humans have different amounts of the power. People with the largest amounts of the divine power are those with the oldest souls. We pay for the mistakes of any given life in the life that follows it.

Students should discuss the following case study among group members according to each person's assigned worldview. Each group should present their decisions and their means of arriving at them. Read all of the worldviews to the class. Discuss difficulties encountered, or would be encountered, in similar situations outside the classroom.

Case Study: A young boy was rescued from a raft floating in the Atlantic Ocean between Cuba and the United States. The boy and his mother were among other Cuban's trying to escape to Florida. Everyone except the boy died in the attempt. The rescued boy was brought to a hospital and his relatives living in Miami were notified. His U.S. relatives, many of whom escaped from Cuba for a better life in the U.S., want him to remain with them. The boy's father, who lives in Cuba, wants his son to come home, to live with him and his current wife. The refugee's mother is dead, and he barely escaped his own death. After his terrible ordeal, he is now in a strange country away from familiar friends, family, and an environment—all part of the fabric of his life. What needs to be done?

Source: Adapted from Ludwig, S. K. & Vrchota, D. A. (1996). *Instructor's resource manual and test bank for Beebe, Beebe, and Redmond's Interpersonal communication: Relating to others.* Needham Heights, MA: Allyn & Bacon.

Film Analysis

Instructions: Choose a film that illustrates another cultural orientation. Ask students to write a description of the following aspects represented in the film on a separate sheet of paper.

1. Description of Culture

2. Language

3. Attributions

4. Cultural Relationship with:

   a. God

   b. Environment

   c. Others

   d. Materialism

   e. Ownership

   f. Time

Case Study: Understanding Cultural Differences

Rationale: In the Thai culture, one of the hardest things to understand and reconcile is the dual attitude of *group harmony*, an emphasis on preserving the good feelings of everyone at all costs (e.g., telling you what they think you want to hear even if it stretches the truth), and a sense of *individualism* or *noninvolvement*, which says that a person is responsible only to him/herself and that one's actions are no one else's concern. (The word *thai* means free; and although it refers to national independence, it is a characteristic of the individual as well.) Thus, Thais are not inclined to accept discipline or regimentation, but at the same time they place great value on keeping relationships pleasant.

This attitude is reflected in the expression *mai pen rai*, which, according to one scholar, signifies "the Thai desire to keep relationships peaceful and on an even keel, to shrug off the little frustrations and disagreements of life, to present anger or passion from coming to the surface."

A related value in the Thai way of life is the concept of *sanuke*, which means "to enjoy oneself." Life is meant to be enjoyed; problems should not stand in the way of this enjoyment. Since Buddhism teaches them to accept their fate, when faced with a problem Thais tend to laugh it off—*mai pen rai.*

Discuss: How does this concept affect John, who is working in Thailand. John may want to first acknowledge and try to understand this cultural difference—that getting the job done on time, within budget, etc., is not the same importance to Thais as to Westerners in general and to people from the United States in particular—and then try to arrive at a solution that will be acceptable to both John and his co-workers. His employees may wish to teach John about Thai culture and why they are accustomed to certain work habits.

Adapted from *The bridge: A review of cross-cultural affairs and international training.* Denver: Center for Research and Education.

Returning Home: My Fellow Americans

Objective: To illustrate that the attitudes of a sojourner change when he or she lives in another culture and that some of these changes may have repercussions upon returning home.

Instructions: Divide the students into groups. Distribute *Returnee Voices* (pp. 62–63). Ask students to read and discuss the "voices" with the other members of their groups. Have each group select a spokesperson to report on the group's reactions.

Facilitator questions:

1. Was the overall reaction to the sojourners' voices positive or negative? Why?
2. Which of the returnee voices do you most identify with? Why?
3. How would you deal with a returnee who is upset about U.S. culture?
4. How would you deal with an international student (not someone from the U.S.) who appears entirely negative about the U.S.?
5. What are the advantages of maintaining a negative attitude toward your home country when you are a sojourner? Examples: In settings where anti-Americanism is rampant, this may be judicious. In adopting an anti-American stance, you may avoid some of the stereotypes the hosts have of Americans. Trying to adopt the attitudes of your hosts is a way to focus on the target culture and, therefore, learn more. Do you think this will change the hosts' view of the American?
6. What are the weaknesses of having a negative attitude toward your home culture? Examples: You may not be entirely fair in your judgment. When you return home, you may alienate everybody. You risk slipping into a denial of your own identity; it is healthier, perhaps, to acknowledge your *Americanism* as well as your skepticism.
7. Do you think these sojourners are just in a stage of culture shock? What may be the next stage?

continued

Returnee Voices

Immediate and initial shock. I hated coming back. The first day—getting into Chicago—I didn't even want to be there. I got into the van and I was yelling at the driver to slow down because I thought he was driving too fast. Everything seemed to be flying by. The driver stopped at a Burger King or something and I didn't feel like going in at all.

Things have changed. I was struck by how many things had happened that I didn't know about. I was almost mad in a way—like, "Why didn't you guys tell me?"

Nobody understands. I was angry with my parents and with everybody else for not understanding why I was depressed. I just cried at the drop of a hat, and they didn't understand, but I didn't know how to explain to them. They were tired of listening to all my stories. (And I could never make the stories sound the way they really were!) It was frustrating.

I'm homesick . . . but I'm home. I cried and cried on the plane and on the bus. . . . I didn't want to come back, and so when I saw my parents, it was nice meeting them, but my mind was still back in [my host country]. . . . After a certain point my parents and friends didn't want to hear about it anymore, and I had absolutely no one to talk to.

Some people are so naive. Many people view China as Red China, ideology China, but when I think of China, I think of my students. It makes me mad when people say stuff like "You couldn't go many places, could you?" or The KGB watched you, didn't they?" The KGB? This is China, not Russia.

Am I happy to be an American? Once I got to the United States, I was repulsed. The grocery store was the worst. I walked in and counted over a hundred different kinds of pop and more than that many kinds of breakfast cereal. It made me sick because it just isn't necessary. I was amazed at how much excess we have and how I had never even thought of it as excess.

continued

Life at home bores me. I was sitting around one day after I got home. It was a cold December day. I think it was drizzling. I was so tired of lying around. My overseas travels were such a big adventure and all of a sudden I had nothing to look forward to except going back to school. I remember getting up, putting on some sweats, and just running. All of a sudden I realized that this was cathartic and I ran as fast as I could—ran and ran and ran.

Why do I feel like this? Part of reentry shock is feeling guilty about my overseas experience—feeling like mine wasn't as good as other people's—and maybe I didn't like it as much as I should have—and maybe I didn't have the best attitude all the time—and feeling like somehow I failed.

Source: Adapted from Hess, J. D. (1994). Returning home (pp. 243–250). *The whole world guide to culture learning*. Yarmouth, ME: Intercultural.

An Asian View of Cultural Differences

We live in time	You live in space.
We are always at rest.	You are always on the move.
We are passive.	You are aggressive.
We like to contemplate.	You like to act.
We accept the world as it is.	You try to change it according to your blueprint.
We live in peace with nature.	You try to impose your will on her.
Religion is our first love.	Technology is your passion.
We delight to think about the meaning of life.	You delight in physics.
We believe in freedom of silence.	You believe in freedom of speech.
We lapse into meditation.	You strive for articulation.
We marry first, then love.	You love first, then marry.
Our marriage is the beginning of a love affair.	Your marriage is the happy end of a romance.
It is an indissoluble bond.	It is a contract.
Our love is mute.	Your love is vocal.
We try to conceal it from the world.	You delight in showing it to others.
Self-denial is a secret to our survival.	Self-assertiveness is the key to your success.
We are taught from the cradle want less and less.	You are urged every day to want more and to more.
We glorify austerity and renunciation.	You emphasize gracious living and enjoyment.
Poverty is to use a badge of spiritual elevation.	Poverty is to you a sign of degradation.
In the sunset years of life we renounce the world and prepare for the hereafter.	You retire early to enjoy the fruits of your labor.

Source: Dr. Mai Van Trang, Vietnam.

Skills That Make a Difference

Rationale: Some people adjust to other cultures more easily then others. There are certain skills or traits that you may have—or, with a little effort, may develop—which will facilitate your adjustment. They are usually attitudes, ways of responding, and styles of behaving.

Instructions: Ask students first, on a scale of one (low) to five (high), to rate themselves on each of the following characteristics. Second, have them circle the traits they think are most important.

____ 1. Tolerance for ambiguity

____ 2. Low goal/task orientation

____ 3. Open-mindedness

____ 4. Nonjudgmentalness

____ 5. Empathy

____ 6. Communicativeness

____ 7. Flexibility; adaptability

____ 8. Curiosity

____ 9. Sense of humor

____ 10. Warmth in human relationships

____ 11. Motivation

____ 12. Self-reliance

____ 13. Strong sense of self

____ 14. Tolerance for differences

____ 15. Perceptiveness

____ 16. Ability to fail

- Scores above 55 indicate a higher degree of adaptability.
- Most important traits: (1) sense of humor, (2) low goal/task orientation, and (3) ability to fail.

Source: Kohls, L. R. (1996). *Survival kit for overseas living.* Yarmouth, MA: Intercultural.

Entertainment-Education

Rationale: *Entertainment education* is the process of designing and implementing media messages to both entertain and educate. These messages are used for the purpose of increasing an audience's knowledge about an educational issue, creating favorable attitudes, and changing overt behavior. This process utilizes the universal appeal of entertainment to persuade individuals to adopt behaviors that will lead to safer and healthier lives. Combining entertainment with education has existed for thousands of years, but the conscious use of the entertainment-education approach in mass communication is a relatively recent phenomenon.

Instructions: Entertainment education has raised such social issues as drunk driving, gay and lesbian rights, AIDS, child abuse, infant mortality, and drug abuse. Provide relevant examples of media messages that have   had a positive impact on social problems: (1) in the United States, and (2) in developing countries.

Singhal, A. & Rogers, E. M. (1999). *Entertainment-Education: A communication strategy for social change.* Mahwah, NJ: Lawrence Erlbaum.

Ethics of Changing Someone Else's Culture

Class Discussion: In chapter 9, *The Global Village*, the *Ethics of Changing Someone Else's Culture* provides the grounds for an important class discussion of ethics. When is purposeful change of another culture justified? Are all attempts to improve the socioeconomic status of economically developing peoples justified? Are arguments against economic development, which destroys traditional cultures, simply arguments to keep the poor, poor?

PART IV

Examination Questions

Chapter One: Context and Contact

Multiple Choice Questions

1. Intercultural communication studies the exchange of information: (pp. 1–2)
   a. between two different cultures.
   b. between different departments of communication in different countries.
   c. between two representatives of a culture.
   d. between two individuals who are culturally unalike.*
   e. between two similar cultures.

2. When a person is ethnocentric he or she is likely to: (p. 2)
   a. think that everything revolves around him/her.
   b. judge other cultures as superior to his/her own culture.
   c. judge other cultures as inferior to his/her own culture.*
   d. think that everything revolves around the ethnolook.
   e. judge other cultures to be like his/her own culture.

3. A person who is afraid of everything foreign, strange, and different is: (p. 2)
   a. claustrophobic.
   b. ethnophobic.
   c. misanthropic.
   d. xenophobic.*
   e. culturalphobic.

4. An embedded memory of historical events that are particularly significant to a given cultural group is: (p. 3)
   a. a common cultural attitude.
   b. a collective cultural consciousness.*
   c. a collective cultural attitude.
   d. a worldview.
   e. a collective vision.

5. The fabric silk has a special significance for intercultural communication. What is it: (pp. 4–5)

a. It was two Persian monks living in China who first brought silk to Europe and allowed for silk production in Constantinople, which in turn ended the Chinese monopoly on silk.
b. It was a very precious, rare commodity and therefore required extraordinary bargaining skills in different languages.
c. It established the silk road, which allowed for more exchange between East and West, not only of commerce, but also of religions and the first vague knowledge of other cultures.*
d. It was a great amount of silk that a Chinese emperor from the Han Dynasty gave to the Greek Emperor Alexander the Great on his visit to China in 360 B.C. and thereby established cultural exchange.
e. all of the above.

6. In the Middle Ages, Spanish culture was strongly influenced by which of the following religious minorities: (p. 7)
a. Buddhists.
b. Jews.
c. Muslims.
d. Moors.*
e. Christians.

7. The main reason for the Crusades was: (pp. 8–11)
a. a speech by Pope Urban II.*
b. the fear of the nobility that the energies of the knights could be turned against them.
c. the worry of Emperor Alexius I that the Turks would threaten his territories around Constantinople.
d. an attack by Muslims on Christians living in Jerusalem.
e. to convert atheists.

8. The speech Pope Urban II delivered at Cluny is considered a modern example of a: (pp. 8–11)
a. sermon.
b. motivational speech.
c. hate speech.*

d. twisting argument.
e. positive rhetoric.

9. One view of Christians in the Middle East was established during the Crusades. It regarded the members of Christianity as: (pp. 8–11)
    a. culturally and militarily superior.
    b. bloodthirsty and murderers of innocent victims.*
    c. anti-Semitic.
    d. intolerant of other religions and cultures.
    e. antiatheist.

10. The holy war of Muslims against Christian Crusaders that is still an important means of recognition and power in Islamic countries today is called: (p. 12)
    a. Hegira.
    b. Jihad.*
    c. Haj.
    d. Koran.
    e. Crusaders.

11. What was one of the main differences between the army of Genghis Khan and any army of his contemporaries: (pp. 12–14)
    a. Genghis Khan's army consisted of drilled fighters in highly coordinated units.
    b. Genghis Khan's army had the advantage of being on horseback, they regarded the Chinese who were not riding like them as sissies.
    c. Genghis Khan's army went to war as a nation, the families going along with the fighting men.*
    d. Genghis Khan's army was the first to use gunpowder.
    e. Genghis Khan's army considered conquering others as noble.

12. The main difference between Kublai Khan and his grandfather Genghis Khan was that Kublai: (p. 17)
    a. pillage and burned all cities he conquered.
    b. established a communication system similar to the pony express and therefore had faster access to any information.

c. taught the civilized Europeans a lesson that made them doubt their assumed superiority.

d. wanted to build and to integrate what he had learned from his Chinese tutors.*

e. wanted to conquer more territory than Genghis.

13. The illustrated edition of the *Travels of Marco Polo* was: (pp. 20–21)

a. regarded as a completely fictional report.

b. seen as an assimilation of facts.

c. met by some with disbelief, while it convinced others of its accuracy.*

d. without any impact on the Western world due to its low numbered edition.

e. not relevant in the literate world.

14. What does the Treaty of Tordesillas illustrate: (p. 21)

a. the misunderstanding of world geography.

b. the colonists' overestimation of their own importance in the world.

c. the settlement of ownership claims of the New World.

d. all of the above.*

e. none of the above.

15. When the Spanish conquistador Hernán Cortés invaded the Aztec capital, the Aztec King Montezuma: (p. 22)

a. gave Cortés his daughter, La Malincha, as a present.

b. treated Cortés as a special guest, because he believed that a god would come from the east.*

c. converted to Christianity.

d. took him and his soldiers under arrest.

e. did nothing because this event never occurred.

16. The first Christian nation to enter slave trade was/were: (pp. 24–27)

a. Denmark.

b. Great Britain.

c. Portugal.*

d. American Colonies.
e. The Americas.

17. The trade process of which the slave trade was part is also known as: (pp. 24–27)
    a. triangle trade.*
    b. the first modern trade logistics.
    c. slaves-for-guns trade.
    d. the initial passage.
    e. the final passage.

18. The term propaganda has its origins in: (p. 28)
    a. the Catholic Congregation for the Propagation of the Faith.*
    b. the Soviet Agency for Agitation and Propaganda.
    c. the German use of information in World War I.
    d. the Inquisition.
    e. the New World.

19. What exchange of goods took place between the Chinese and British merchants in the 19th century: (pp. 29–30)
    a. porcelain for silver.
    b. spices for silver.
    c. opium for silver.
    d. goods for opium.*
    e. silver for silk.

20. The reason for the elimination of the Permanent Indian Territory starting in the middle of the last century was: (pp. 32–36)
    a. the urge by settlers to remove the Indian threat.
    b. the divine determination that the United States should be one nation from coast to coast.*
    c. the fact that the Native Americans could not adapt to the new American culture.
    d. the discovery that the Indian Territory was prime farm land.
    e. the discovery that the Indian Territory was prime grazing land.

True/False Questions

1. Culture reveals more than it hides. (F, p. 3)

2. One of the achievements of the Silk Road was that it brought clear and detailed knowledge of cultures in the East. (F, p. 5)

3. The prejudice of regarding people from the Middle East as Muslim infidels has lasted from the crusades until today. (T, p. 12)

4. Ogadai Khan established a communication system in the 13th century that was not surpassed in efficiency for another six centuries. (T, p. 15)

5. Asian countries were associated only with desirable goods and technologies and never regarded as the source of deadly diseases. (F, p. 21)

6. The Americas were originally divided up by Spain and France. (F, p. 21)

7. The Cherokee Nation completely adapted to American culture in less than 30 years and was therefore the only Indian Tribe not forced to give up their land. (F, p. 22)

8. The cultural diversity of modern life is a strength of today's society. (T, p. 38)

Essay Questions

1. Discuss in detail one historic example of intercultural communication.

2. Explain the following terms in your own words and give an example for each: ethnocentric, xenophobic, collective cultural consciousness.

3. Historic instances of intercultural communication can be divided roughly into three categories, according to the main reason behind them: Economic, political or religious. Pick one example from each of the three categories and elaborate on it.

4. Compare the three great Khan rulers and the changes from one generation to the next.

5. Compare two instances of intercultural communication, driven by either religious or economic reasons.

6. What are current instances of intercultural communication? Give three examples, explain how they work and elaborate on why you think they are successful or unsuccessful.

Chapter Two: The Study of Intercultural Communication

Multiple Choice Questions

1. Intercultural communication owes much of its first theoretical basis to the German Sociologist: (pp. 39–40)
    a. Albion Small.
    b. Max Weber.
    c. Georg Simmel.*
    d. Robert E. Park.
    e. Sigmund Freud.

2. Cultural heterophily plays an important role in the concept of: (pp. 40–43)
    a. xenophilia.
    b. the stranger.*
    c. the culturally dissimilar.
    d. people from similar cultural backgrounds.
    e. both a and b.

3. A stranger is: (pp. 40–43)
    a. in the situation of representing an exciting, alluring, and attractive person, due to his status.
    b. sometimes disliked.
    c. mostly feared because of the apparent and assumed differences.
    d. often the foundation upon which fiction is built.
    e. all of the above.*

4. The degree to which an individual perceives a lack of intimacy with individuals different in ethnicity, race, religion, occupation, etc., is also known as: (p. 44)
    a. the concept of the stranger.
    b. the concept of marginal man.
    c. the concept of social distance.*
    d. the concept of heterophily.
    e. the concept of xenophobia.

5. According to Robert E. Park, an individual who lives in two different worlds is a part of the concept of: (p. 45)
    a. marginal man.*
    b. heterophily.
    c. the traveler.
    d. the stranger.
    e. none of the above.

6. Heterophily is defined as: (pp. 45–46)
    a. the degree to which two or more individuals who communicate are alike.
    b. the degree to which the communication of two or more individuals is alike.
    c. the degree to which two or more individuals who communicate are unalike.*
    d. the degree to which we maintain a different opinion.
    e. the degree to which two kinds of communication are unalike.

7. Individuals who have a relatively high degree of communication outside of their own system and thus provide the superordinated system with openness are: (pp. 46–47)
    a. travelers.
    b. strangers.
    c. localities.
    d. nationalities.
    e. cosmopolites.*

8. There are several concepts that have been influenced by the concept of the stranger. Which is the correct time sequence (earliest first): (pp. 46–47)
    a. heterophily, social distance, cosmopoliteness, marginal man.
    b. social distance, marginal man, cosmopoliteness, heterophily.*
    c. marginal man, social distance, cosmopoliteness, heterophily.
    d. social distance, cosmopoliteness, heterophily, marginal man.
    e. heterophily, marginal man, social distance, cosmopoliteness.

9. The affiliation with which of the following groups leads an individual to take on the group's values as an ideal and as an instrument to judge others: (p. 49)
   a. affiliation with outgroups.
   b. affiliation with parties.
   c. affiliation with churches.
   d. affiliation with ingroups.*
   e. affiliation with cults.

10. Ethnocentrism allows people to: (pp. 50–51)
   a. judge other cultures on the basis of their perceived superiority.
   b. judge other cultures on the basis of their perceived inferiority.*
   c. judge other cultures on the basis of objectivity.
   d. judge other cultures on the basis of scientific inquiry.
   e. none of the above.

11. The context of a culture plays a significant role in: (p. 55)
   a. cultural relativism.*
   b. cosmopoliteness.
   c. prejudice.
   d. discrimination.
   e. ingroups.

12. The affiliation with ingroups leads to the formation of: (pp. 55–56)
   a. political doctrines.
   b. dogmas.
   c. prejudice.*
   d. cultural relativism.
   e. cultural correctness.

13. Which of the following is a generalization about a group of people that oversimplifies reality: (p. 58)
   a. prejudice.
   b. dogma.
   c. statistics.
   d. survey.
   e. stereotype.*

14. Which scale in the theory of the authoritarian personality measures the degree of prejudice of an individual: (p. 58)
    a. the b-scale.
    b. the d-scale.
    c. the f-scale.*
    d. the p-scale.
    e. the x-scale.

15. The main reason for the failure of development programs in Third World nations in the time after the Second World War has to do with: (p. 60)
    a. the kind of technology that was introduced.
    b. the fact that the programs were not well funded.
    c. the quality of the personnel working in the program.
    d. the primitive condition in most nations.
    e. the way the programs were implemented.*

16. The Foreign Service Institute's primary task was: (pp. 62–63)
    a. recruiting of personnel for development programs.
    b. language training of the United States Army.
    c. intercultural education of government officials.
    d. pre- and in-service training of Foreign Service officers.*
    e. all of the above.

17. An anthropologist with extensive intercultural experience who led the training courses at the Foreign Service Institute: (pp. 63–66)
    a. George Simmel.
    b. Robert E. Park.
    c. Edward T. Hall. *
    d. Benjamin Lee Whorf.
    e. Thomas Steinfatt.

18. The two nonverbal forms of communication studied by the Foreign Service Institute were chronemics (the use of time) and: (pp. 67–68)
    a. kinetics.
    b. phonemics.
    c. phonetics.

d. proxemics.*

e. acoustics.

19. What is a scientific paradigm: (pp. 70–74)
    a. a conceptualization offering solutions to a research question.
    b. a conceptualization providing exemplary problems and methods of research.*
    c. a conceptualization defining a scientific problem.
    d. a conceptualization forming a research hypothesis and test questions.
    e. none of the above.

20. The evolution of a new scientific paradigm involves preparadigm research, appearance of a new paradigm, normal science, anomaly, and: (pp. 70–74)
    a. result.
    b. exhaustion.*
    c. solution.
    d. definition
    e. research hypothesis.

True/False Questions

1. The concept of the stranger was first defined by Edward T. Hall. (F, p. 40)

2. Homophily is the degree to which two or more individuals who communicate are alike. (T, p. 45)

3. Maps using the Mercator projection are usually Eurocentric and grossly distort land areas. (T, p. 51)

4. Stereotypes are highly descriptive representations of an average group. (F, p. 58)

5. The ethnocentrism scale developed by Adorno after World War II also measured prejudice and fascist tendencies. (F, p. 58)

6. The United States had the most effective diplomats, because each candidate held a degree from an Ivy League University and had excellent skills in foreign languages. (F, p. 62)

7. Chronemics is the term Edward Hall coined for nonverbal communication that involves time. (T, p. 67)

8. Prejudice is an unfounded attitude toward an outgroup based on a comparison with one's ingroup. (T, p. 76)

Essay Questions

1. Define the following terms in your own words: Prejudice, racism, reverse discrimination, nonverbal communication, proxemics, and paradigm.

2. Outline the development of intercultural communication as a study from its beginning to the 1950s.

3. Describe the five concepts Georg Simmel and Robert E. Park developed that deal with the interpersonal relationships an individual has with other individuals or with a larger system of which she or he is a part.

4. List four of the eight critical concepts in intercultural communication, define them, and provide examples.

5. Describe the five stages that establish a new scientific paradigm.

6. Elaborate on the changes in intercultural communication after World War II, in particular the development of the Foreign Service Institute and the significance of Edward T. Hall.

Chapter Three: Culture

Multiple Choice Questions

1. Culture consists of: (pp. 79–81):
    a. learned and shared behavior patterns.
    b. the total way of life of a people.
    c. values and norms.
    d. all of the above.*
    e. none of the above.

2. What is a co-culture: (pp. 79–81)
    a. a second culture existing along side a first culture.
    b. a similar culture found in a different environment.
    c. a set of shared cultural meanings held by a system within a system.*
    d. two equally significant cultures in human development.
    e. b and d.

3. What is a belief: (pp. 81–82)
    a. an individual's perception of a higher being.
    b. an individual's representation of the outside world.*
    c. a culturally determined perception of a higher being.
    d. a culturally determined perception of the outside world.
    e. a culturally preconceived notion.

4. Attitudes are: (pp. 81–82)
    a. internal events not directly observable by other people.*
    b. internal processes triggered by a certain event.
    c. irrational processes triggered by a certain event.
    d. irrational events not directly observable by other people.
    e. all of the above.

5. People who share a culture use _____ to regard something as good or bad. (pp. 81–82)
    a. beliefs.
    b. attitudes.
    c. perceptions.

d. stereotypes.

e. values.*

6. The unique quality of a cultural belief is: (p. 82)
   a. that members who share a culture have more similar beliefs than individuals of different cultures.*
   b. that every member in a society holds exactly the same cultural beliefs.
   c. that it can be used to judge an occurring phenomenon on a basis that all members sharing the culture hold the same belief.
   d. that all other individual beliefs are considered inferior.
   e. that all other individual beliefs are considered superior.

7. The significant aspect of cultural values is that they: (pp. 84–85)
   a. involve judgment.
   b. are parsimonious.
   c. are normative.
   d. a and b.
   e. a and c.*

8. An established behavior pattern for members of a social system is also known as: (p. 85)
   a. a set of rules.
   b. a set of norms.*
   c. a code of behavior.
   d. a code of laws.
   e. all of the above.

9. What is the main difference between an individualistic and collectivistic culture: (pp. 86–89)
   a. In an individualistic culture the goals of the collectivity are valued over those of the individual.
   b. In a collectivistic culture the goals of the individual are valued over those of the collectivity.
   c. In an individualistic culture the goals of the individual are of lesser importance than those of the collectivity.

d. In a collectivistic culture the goals of the individual are of lesser importance than those of the collectivity.*

e. In a collectivistic culture the goals of the collectivity are of lesser importance than those of the individual.

10. The nature of the self is: (p. 89)
    a. to see oneself as independent in individualistic cultures and as connected to others in collectivistic cultures.
    b. shaped by one's culture.
    c. determined by one's communication.
    d. formed by one's perceptions.
    e. all of the above.*

11. A high-context culture is defined as: (pp. 90–95)
    a. one in which the meanings of a communication message are stated clearly and explicitly.
    b. one in which the meanings of a communication message found in the situation or are internalized in the communicators.*
    c. one in which verbalized messages are more important than unverbalized messages.
    d. all of the above.
    e. none of the above.

12. Which of the following statements are true: (pp. 90–95)
    a. It is easier for a high-context person to talk to a low-context person than vice versa.
    b. It is easier for a low-context person to talk to a high-context person than vice versa.
    c. There are no difficulties in the talk situation for either side.
    d. Both sides have different difficulties talking to each other.*
    e. There are no situations in which the two cultures communicate at all.

13. Cultural tendencies exist: (pp. 95–96)
    a. only within a given group or culture.
    b. only between different cultures.
    c. and can vary with the individual.

d. only to a certain degree and differences can often be attributed to social class and socioeconomic status.

e. all of the above.*

14. The conflict that occurs between two or more cultures when they disagree about a certain value is generally known as: (pp. 96–97)

a. a culture clash.*

b. a cultural conflict.

c. a cultural crash.

d. a cultural shock.

e. a culture war.

15. The practice of clitorectomy in the United States and the reaction it arouses is an example of: (pp. 96–97)

a. culture shock.

b. culture clash.*

c. cultural identification.

d. cultural markers.

e. cultural differences.

16. A physical appearance and a name that suggests a cultural identity are termed: (pp. 100–101)

a. cultural identifiers.

b. cultural markers.*

c. cultural differences.

d. ethnic identifiers.

e. ethnic markers.

17. Another element important for cultural identification is: (pp. 102–103)

a. the place of birth.

b. the country living in during childhood.

c. the country living in during adulthood.

d. the language.*

e. the nationality.

18. Which of the following is NOT a form of cultural difference? (p. 103)
    a. gender.
    b. age.
    c. religion.
    d. socioeconomic status.
    e. none of the above.*

19. Intercultural differences can best be arranged: (pp. 105–108)
    a. in a circle.
    b. on a continuum.*
    c. in a triangle.
    d. on a map.
    e. not at all.

20. The significance of Elvis Presley can be found in his: (p. 109)
    a. cultural difference.
    b. cultural identification.
    c. cultural shareability.*
    d. culture shock.
    e. culture war.

True/False Questions

1. Each different group or population creates its own way of life, with the values, norms, behaviors, and material objects that they feel best fit their situation. (T, p. 81)

2. Attitudes and beliefs indicate behavioral intentions, tendencies for a person to respond to events, ideas, and people in particular ways. (T, p. 81)

3. Everyone in a society holds exactly the same cultural beliefs. (F, p. 82)

4. In collectivistic cultures, individual privacy is extremely important. (F, p. 87)

5. Edward T. Hall originated the classification of high-context versus low-context cultures on the basis of the amount of information that is directly stated in a message. (T. p. 90)

6. Culture clashes frequently occur in cities that are composed of a homogenous ethnic group. (F, p. 97)

7. Culture markers, such as culturally identifiable names and physical appearance, are 100 percent reliable in predicting cultural identification. (F, pp. 100–101)

8. As the degree of intercultural difference becomes wider in human communication situations, information exchange is likely to be more effective. (F, p. 106)

Essay Questions

1. What is culture? Define culture in a way that the concept is most useful for the study of intercultural communication. Be specific about what you would leave in and what you would exclude from the concept.

2. The case of the Hmong spirits suggests that the consideration of cultural beliefs is important in intercultural communication. Suppose someone argued that the consideration of such beliefs amounts to the sanctioning of irrationality. How would you respond?

3. Define and contrast the concepts of collectivistic versus individualistic cultures and discuss their utility in intercultural communication.

4. Define and contrast the concepts of high context and low context cultures and discuss their utility in intercultural communication.

5. Discuss the following idea and its implications for intercultural communication: The variations within a culture

may account for as much or more of the variation in intercultural interpretations of messages as does the differences between cultures.

6. Discuss the concept of cultural identification in terms of language and cultural markers.

Chapter Four: Communication

Multiple Choice Questions

1. Meanings are in: (p. 113)
    a. words.
    b. people.*
    c. symbols.
    d. senders.
    e. environment.

2. The fact that communication is ubiquitous means that it is: (pp. 113–114)
    a. difficult to understand.
    b. very selective.
    c. involved in every aspect of daily life.*
    d. simple and easy to use.
    e. usually taken for granted.

3. The altering influence on a message in the communication process is called: (pp. 114–117)
    a. feedback.
    b. channel.
    c. decoding.
    d. noise.*
    e. distortion.

4. A message about the effects of a previous message that is sent back to the source is: (p. 115)
    a. noise.
    b. channel.
    c. perceptions.
    d. feedback.*
    e. encoding.

5. The change in an individual's knowledge, attitudes, and overt behavior due to exposure to a communication message is called: (pp. 114–117)
    a. feedback.

b. noise.

c. effect.*

d. information.

e. subjectivity of communication.

6. Why was the code used by the United States Marines during World War II one of the few unbreakable ones: (pp. 114–117)

    a. The code-talkers used a computer-developed system.

    b. The code-talkers used an almost extinct Samoan dialect.

    c. The code-talkers used the names of dinosaurs and geological terms that were given a different meaning.

    d. The code-talkers used a Dakota Sioux dialect.

    e. The code-talkers used the Navajo language Diné.*

7. An individual's inability to predict or to understand some situation due to a lack of information about alternatives is: (p. 120)

    a. semantic.

    b. feedback.

    c. noise.

    d. attribution.

    e. uncertainty.*

8. Beginning a conversation with a complete stranger is difficult because: (pp. 120–125)

    a. of the standard parent sentence: "Don't talk to strangers."

    b. one usually does not know what to talk about or how to begin.

    c. of one's inability to predict or understand a situation without having any information.*

    d. the other person often looks weird and makes no effort to start a conversation.

    e. there is usually nothing the other person and oneself could have in common.

9. In communication, the antidote for uncertainty is: (pp. 120–125)

    a. certainty.

    b. knowledge.

    c. proof.

d. information.*

e. discourse.

10. Intrapersonal communication is defined as: (pp. 125–126)
    a. occurring inside of one person.*
    b. occurring mainly at the workplace and in school.
    c. occurring mainly between good friends.
    d. occurring mainly in families.
    e. all of the above.

11. The process of exchanging mutually understood symbols in a
    face-to-face exchange of information is commonly known as:
    (pp. 125–126)
    a. communication.
    b. interpersonal communication.*
    c. intrapersonal communication.
    d. intimate personal communication.
    e. interim communication.

12. A physical event or action that directly represents something
    else is a: (p. 126)
    a. denominator.
    b. sign.*
    c. key.
    d. symbol.
    e. fixed meaning.

13. The use of vocalized sounds, written symbols representing
    these sounds or ideas, and grammatical rules organizing the
    patterns is also known as: (pp. 126–128)
    a. symbolic code.
    b. key.
    c. message.
    d. language.*
    e. all of the above.

14. The key to deciphering the hieroglyphics was the 1799
    discovery of the: (pp. 126–128)

a. papyrus rolls that charted the exact equivalent of Greek letters in Egyptian hieroglyphics.
b. Stone of Wisdom.
c. tomb of King Ptolomy V.
d. Egyptian dictionary in a grave in the Egyptian city of the dead, Necropolis.
e. Rosetta Stone.*

15. The meaning of a word is something inherent to: (pp. 128–129)
    a. symbols.
    b. all world languages.
    c. person using the word.*
    d. word itself.
    e. dictionaries.

16. According to Rogers and Steinfatt, how many levels of meaning can be extracted from the analysis of a communication process: (pp. 129–130)
    a. 1–5.
    b. 1–10.
    c. 1–6.
    d. 0–6.
    e. 0–5.*

17. The syntactic meaning rests on the: (pp. 129–130)
    a. intention of the communication.
    b. alternative scenario.
    c. grammatical structure of a language.*
    d. general composition of the language's vocabulary.
    e. prior condition of meaning.

18. The process in which an individual explains the meaning of others' behavior based on the individual's own experiences, values, and beliefs is called: (p. 131)
    a. acceptance.
    b. tolerance.
    c. assumption.

d. attribution.*

e. actual intent.

19. The degree to which one party controls resources valued by another party is called: (p. 133)
    a. party politics.
    b. supremacy.
    c. superiority.
    d. power.*
    e. priority.

True/False Questions

1. The models and concepts of communication are the same for intercultural communication as they are for other types of communication. (T, p. 113).

2. Encoding is the process by which the physical message is converted into an idea by the receiver. (F, 114)

3. Uncertainty is an individual's ability to predict or to understand some situation due to a lack of information about alternatives. (F, p. 121)

4. Signs are something that represents something else through prior agreement. (F, p. 126)

5. The meanings of a message are interpreted through a process in which the message content is interfaced with an individual's feelings, prior experiences, and cultural values. (T, p. 128)

6. Communication can only transmit meaning, not create meaning. (F, p. 128)

7. A fundamental element in attribution is: *My* actions are in response to what happens to me in the environment and *your* actions are due to the kind of person you are. (F, p. 131)

8. The role of power in communication can be neglected, as the effectiveness of the communication depends on other factors, such as channel, noise and feedback. (F, p. 133)

Essay Questions

1. Discuss what factors helped the Navajo Code-Talkers implement an effective secret message system.

2. When Drew asked Rika to go to the Rat and she responded "no," explain what was happening in meaning assignment within each person.

3. How does the deciphering of the Rosetta Stone relate to the concept that meanings are in people?

4. The Levels of Meaning model describes five levels. What is the importance of this model for intercultural communication?

5. The concept that meaning are in people implies that people must attribute meaning to all messages and to any observations that are to become meaningful to them. How is this attributional process especially important in intercultural settings and interactions?

6. Discuss the incident involving the Nepalese Crown Prince and Pakistani engineers in Thailand. What intercultural variables were involved in this misunderstanding?

Chapter Five: Verbal Communication

Multiple Choice Questions

1. The degree to which language influences human thought is called: (pp. 135–140)
   a. intrapersonal communication.
   b. interpersonal communication.
   c. nonverbal communication.
   d. verbal communication.
   e. linguistic relativity.*

2. As suggested by Whorf, to what extent does language have the ability to influence thinking: (pp. 135–140)
   a. Thinking is independent from language abilities.
   b. The higher the degree of education, the lower the ability of language to influence thinking.
   c. Language and thinking are tied together so closely that a person's language determines his categories of thought.*
   d. The relationship of language and thinking is unidirectional; thoughts only influence language.
   e. The categories of thought of an individual are only influenced by language to a certain age.

3. The Whorfian Hyopothesis is also known as: (pp. 135–140)
   a. Aristotle's linguistic view.
   b. linguistic Zeitgeist hypothesis.
   c. nominalist hypothesis.
   d. linguistic Weltanschauung hypothesis.*
   e. hypothesis of linguist influences.

4. The basis for the hypothesis of linguistic relativity was provided by: (pp. 135–140)
   a. Aristotle.
   b. Georg Simmel.
   c. Robert E. Park
   d. Franz Boas.*
   e. Edward Sapir.

5. What is the connection between the hypothesis of linguistic relativity and intercultural communication: (pp. 135–140)
   a. that different cultures cannot communicate because they don't share the same categories of thought.
   b. that a cultural system is embodied in the language of the people who speak the language.*
   c. the fact that speaking different language will enhance thinking.
   d. the fact that different cultures have different language.
   e. there is no connection.

6. Being fluent in a language and using it to communicate is vital to: (pp. 141–144)
   a. empathy.
   b. understanding a culture.
   c. effectively studying nonverbal communication.
   d. a and b.*
   e. a and c.

7. Which signs were changed from English to French in the Canadian province of Québec in order to protect and promote the use of the French language: (pp. 141–144)
   a. highway direction signs.
   b. street name signs.
   c. shop signs.
   d. stop signs.
   e. all of the above.*

8. What is perception: (pp. 145–146)
   a. An individual, not necessarily true view of the world.
   b. A collective, mutually agreed upon view of the world.
   c. A view of the world that does not have any effect on behavior.
   d. The way in which a culture gives meaning to an object.
   e. The way in which an individual gives meaning to an object.*

9. The theory that individuals act toward objects on the basis of meaning and perceptions that are formed through communication with others is called: (p. 148)

a. interpersonal communication.
b. interpersonal theory.
c. communication interaction.
d. linguistic relativity.
e. symbolic interaction.*

10. George Herbert Mead is linked to the development of the theory of: (p. 148)
    a. linguistic relativity.
    b. communication interaction.
    c. symbolic interaction.*
    d. interpersonal communication.
    e. assigning meaning.

11. Code-switching is the process of: (pp. 148–149)
    a. assigning different codes to different forms of communication.
    b. moving from spoken to written language or vice versa.
    c. any change in means of communication, such as spoken, written, sign, or the medium.
    d. any change from one language to another in a conversation.*
    e. moving from a level of formality to informality.

12. What is the main reason that many government funded communication projects aimed at Native Americans were unsuccessful: (pp. 150–151)
    a. Their cultural heritage tells Native Americans that the United States government is not to be trusted.
    b. The value of reticence is very high in many Native American cultures.*
    c. The projects ignored the actual needs of Native Americans.
    d. The means of communicating through telephone is alien to their culture.
    e. The projects were not funded long enough.

13. In a culture with a strong oral tradition, such as the African-American culture, an important factor that distinguishes its communication from that of a culture with a tradition in writing, such as European cultures, is: (p. 151)

a. use of silence.
b. special vocabulary.
c. speaking style.*
d. switching of codes.
e. there is not distinction.

14. The process through which participants in a conversation decide who will talk first, next, and so forth is called: (p. 152)
a. hierarchical order.
b. ranking.
c. significance.
d. turn-taking.*
e. nonverbal communication.

15. "Disclosure begets disclosure" refers to the concept of: (pp. 152–153)
a. encouraging reciprocal disclosure in a communication situation.*
b. disclosing social taboos.
c. concealing personal information from a stranger.
d. cultural appropriateness.
e. none of the above.

16. The two dimensions of a message generally distinguished by communication scholars are the message content (what is said) and: (pp. 153–154)
a. the message receiver (to whom it is said).
b. the message sender (who said it).
c. the message context (when and where it is said).
d. the relationship (how it is said).*
d. all of the above.

17. The communication about communication is called: (pp. 153–154)
a. relationship message.
b. metacommunication.*
c. multicommunication.

d. supracommunication.

e. second level communication.

18. Erving Goffman's book, *The Presentation of Self in Everyday Life*, is concerned with the concept of: (pp. 154–155)

a. image.

b. impression.

c. face.*

d. stage of life.

e. masque.

19. The receiving role in communication is: (p. 157)

a. less significant than the sending role.

b. usually neglected by communication scholars, because it is too simple.

c. twofold, as there are active and passive listeners.*

d. insignificant, because listeners forget 50 percent of a lecture after two weeks.

e. none of the above.

20. Listeners forget _____ percent of a lecture after two weeks. (p. 157)

a. 20

b. 35

c. 50

d. 75*

e. 85

True/False Questions

1. If men define situations as real, they are real in all of their consequences. (T, p. 145)

2. White and African-American teenage girls show no cultural differences in their perception of the right body weight. (F, 146)

3. According to George Herbert Mead, a person is born with a self, which develops instinctively. (F, p. 148)

4. Self-disclosure is an important part of every face-to-face interpersonal exchange. (F, p. 152).

5. Impression is defined as the public self-image that an individual wants to present in a particular social context. (F, p. 154)

6. In Japan, a person's home is very private, and most invitations to dinner involve going to a restaurant. (T, p. 156)

7. The receiving role in the communication process is not as important as the sending role. (F, p. 157)

8. Many difficulties in communication between culturally dissimilar individuals may be due to cultural factors in listening behavior. (T, p. 158)

Essay Questions

1. Define and discuss the concept of linguistic relativity and its importance for intercultural communication.

2. Discuss the role of perceptions in intercultural communication, including their function in symbolic interaction and in code switching.

3. Talk versus silence, and speaking style, are discussed as types of cultural factors in interpersonal communication. What is the relevance of these concepts for intercultural communication?

4. Turn-taking, and self-disclosure, are discussed as types of cultural factors in interpersonal communication. What is the relevance of these concepts for intercultural communication?

5. Content versus relationship, and face, are discussed as types of cultural factors in interpersonal communication. What is the relevance of these concepts for intercultural communication?

6. Discuss the relationship of listening to intercultural communication, including such concepts as active listening.

Chapter Six: Nonverbal Communication

Multiple Choice Questions

1. One major difference between nonverbal and verbal communication is that much nonverbal communication is: (pp. 161–165)
   a. easy to decipher without knowing the code.
   b. a simpler level of communication.
   c. controllable and intentional.
   d. unintentional and unconscious.*
   e. a and b.

2. A synonym for nonverbal communication coined by Edward T. Hall is: (pp. 161–165)
   a. sign language.
   b. silent language.*
   c. three dimensional language.
   d. other dimension of language.
   e. none of the above.

3. Which of the following is a characteristic of nonverbal communication: (pp. 161–165)
   a. Nonverbal communication is omnipresent.
   b. Nonverbal communication usually comes first.
   c. Nonverbal communication is especially trustworthy.
   d. Nonverbal communication is especially important in intercultural communication situations.
   e. all of the above.*

4. One of the first scholars to study the field of nonverbal communication was: (pp. 167–168)
   a. Sigmund Freud.
   b. Charles Darwin.*
   c. Edward Hall.
   d. Raymond Birdwhistell.
   e. Georg Simmel.

5. Which statement can be traced back to the first scholar in nonverbal communication: (pp. 167–168)
    a. Nonverbal communication is unconscious.
    b. Nonverbal communication is a simpler level of communication.
    c. Nonverbal communication is less effective in giving false information.*
    d. Nonverbal communication is universal.
    e. Nonverbal communication is omnipresent.

6. The role of culture in nonverbal communication: (pp. 171–172)
    a. is a minor one.
    b. is a disrupting one.
    c. is that it establishes mutual understanding.
    d. is that it establishes standards for nonverbal behavior.*
    e. is that it decreases the chance of misunderstanding.

7. Another term for body language is: (pp. 172–175)
    a. physical movements.
    b. kinetics.
    c. kinesics.*
    d. physical appearance.
    e. all of the above.

8. Body movements that can be translated into words and that are used intentionally to transmit a message are called: (pp. 172–175)
    a. signals.
    b. symbols.
    c. illustrators.
    d. emblems.*
    e. hand-talk.

9. The type of body language that accompanies what is said verbally is called: (p. 174)
    a. illustrators.*
    b. emblems.

c. sign.
d. symbol.
e. regulator.

10. Nonverbal communication that involves the use of space is called: (pp. 176–179)
    a. chronemics.
    b. kinetics.
    c. kinesics.
    d. proxemics.*
    e. space-talk.

11. The zone of participation is: (pp. 176–179)
    a. the space between two participants in a communication situation.
    b. the seating in a conference room around a table.
    c. the seating in a classroom with eye contact with the teacher.*
    d. the space between individual students in a classroom.
    e. a and d.

12. The way in which time affects communication is called: (p. 181)
    a. chronemics.*
    b. kinetics.
    c. kinesics.
    d. proxemics.
    e. time-talk.

13. In general, culture determines the conventions of: (pp. 182–183)
    a. who may touch whom.
    b. how long to touch.
    c. under which conditions touch may take place.

d. where to touch.

e. a, c, and d.*

14. The part of vocal communication concerned with everything beyond the verbal content is called: (p. 184)
    a. pseudolanguage.
    b. nonverbal language.
    c. nonword communication.
    d. paralanguage.*
    e. all of the above.

15. Personal items and possessions that are used to communicate a message in a communication situation are called: (p. 184)
    a. accessories.
    b. artistic communicators.
    c. artifacts.*
    d. ambient communicators.
    e. material communicators.

16. Physical appearance is an important aspect in intercultural communication on a nonverbal level because: (p. 185)
    a. elements of appearance that are considered physically attractive are dictated by rule-governed cultural preferences.
    b. of its importance for the first impressions between strangers.
    c. members of some cultures are considered more beautiful than others.
    d. physical beauty is only a factor in United States' dating situations.
    e. a and b.*

17. Which of the following is NOT considered a characteristic behavior of individuals when they are lying: (pp. 186–187)
    a. less sincere smiling and more fake smiling.
    b. more blushing and nervous hand rubbing.*
    c. longer pauses.
    d. more blinking and pupil dilation.
    e. more slips of the tongue.

18. Nonverbal communication is not immune to cultural misunderstandings. Between the Japanese and United States people, common misunderstandings occur with the following action: (pp. 186–187)
   a. a handshake.
   b. a smile.
   c. maintaining eye contact.
   d. having a tattoo.
   e. all of the above.*

19. Kinesic behaviors that control turn-taking and other procedural aspects of interpersonal communication are called: (p. 174)
   a. illustrators.
   b. emblems.
   c. affect displays.
   d. proxemics.
   e. regulators.*

20. Much of nonverbal communication is unintentional and _____. (p. 188)
   a. conscious.
   b. unconscious.*
   c. intentional
   d. difficult.
   e. hidden.

True/False Questions

1. Nonverbal communication is defined as all types of communication that take place without words. (T, p. 162).

2. Nonverbal communication can lead to misunderstanding, especially when verbal messages are missing or limited. (T, p. 164)

3. There are no gender differences in using hand gestures, but there are cultural differences. (F, p. 174)

4. How physically close people stand when they talk only tells us about their cultural background and not their personal relationship. (F, p. 176)

5. The nonverbal communication that involves touch is also known as haptics. (T, p. 182)

6. Each one of the indicators of lying has been proven to predict exactly whether a person is lying or not. (F, p. 186)

7. If someone from the United States walks with a slouch, a Japanese person assumes that he or she is part of the Japanese Mafia. (T, p. 187)

8. International negotiator Bill Richardson almost risked the lives of two U.S. citizens by turning his back to Saddam Hussein and walking out of the room. (F, p. 166)

Essay Questions

1. Why is nonverbal communication important in intercultural communication?

2. Discuss the contributions of Darwin, Hall, and Birdwhistell to the nonverbal aspects of intercultural communication.

3. Discuss the various type of body movements that affect intercultural communication.

4. Discuss how space, time, and touch may affect intercultural communication.

5. Discuss how voice, artifacts, and physical appearance may affect intercultural communication.

6. How does nonverbal communication affect cultural misunderstandings? Give two examples, one from your experience and one from the book.

Chapter Seven: Assimilation, Mass Communication, and Sojourning

Multiple Choice Questions

1. The degree to which an individual relinquishes an original culture for another is called: (pp. 190–195)
    a. cultural maintenance.
    b. assimilation.*
    c. code switching.
    d. acculturation.
    e. culture shock.

2. A person who becomes a mixture of two or more cultures has undergone the process of: (pp. 190–195)
    a. code switching.
    b. acculturation.*
    c. culture shock.
    d. assimilation.
    e. polyculturalism.

3. The exponential increase of mass media is associated with: (pp. 190–195)
    a. development of newspapers.
    b. development of magazines.
    c. development of television.
    d. development of the Internet.
    e. none of the above.*

4. One example, given in the book, of the trend away from assimilation toward cultural maintenance is: (pp. 190–195)
    a. the Asian-American community.
    b. the African-American community.
    c. the European immigrant community.
    d. the Latin community.*
    e. the most recent immigrants of any community.

5. The Gypsies managed to remain permanent strangers in any system as a result of: (pp. 190–195)
    a. their disability to comply with the rules.

b. their preference of jobs, such as fortune-telling and circus entertainment.
c. their life of constant traveling.*
d. their unknown cultural origins.
e. their strange habits.

6. The strong presence of different ethnic groups in cities like New York and Los Angeles is best reflected in: (pp. 190–195)
   a. different names in a telephone book.
   b. increasing number of ethnic media.*
   c. difficulty of finding someone who can speak English.
   d. variety of foods offered in a supermarket.
   e. number of languages taught in local schools.

7. Which reason is given for the slowing of the melting-pot process: (pp. 190–195)
   a. the stubbornness of many immigrants who don't want to learn English.
   b. the fact that the number of ethnic media promotes keeping one's original language.
   c. the lack of programs that promote integration.
   d. the fact that many former minority populations have become majorities.*
   e. the decrease of interracial marriages.

8. A typical characteristic of an ethnic group is: (pp. 190–195)
   a. They dress in a similar fashion.
   b. They have a genuine cooking style.
   c. They share a common language.*
   d. They have similar physical features.
   e. none of the above.

9. Language is the most important factor in which of the following developments: (pp. 199–200)
   a. assimilation versus cultural maintenance.*
   b. cultural maintenance versus culture shock.
   c. acculturation versus polyculturalism.
   d. culture shock versus code switching.
   e. b and d.

10. In which will Spanish become more important in the next decades: (pp. 199–200)
    a. as a foreign language in schools.
    b. as a second official language in many southern states in the United States.
    c. as a special code for the Latino population.
    d. as a language for a growing number of television stations and newspapers.*
    e. as a second official language in many countries.

11. People in the United States are less informed about international affairs than people of: (pp. 199–200)
    a. Germany.
    b. England.
    c. France.
    d. Italy.
    e. all of the above.*

12. Which strong bias has been found in the mainstream media: (pp. 199–200)
    a. bias against old people.
    b. bias against young people.
    c. bias against athletes.
    d. bias against women.*
    e. bias against teenagers.

13. An example of a sojourner is: (pp. 211–212)
    a. a person from the United States who works overseas.
    b. an exchange student.
    c. a tourist.
    d. an immigrant.
    e. a, b, and c.*

14. The difficulty of adapting to a new cultural environment is known as: (pp. 212–213)
    a. assimilation.
    b. acculturation.
    c. code witching.
    d. culture shock.*
    e. traumatic experience.

15. The process of adapting to a new cultural environment and returning to the culture of origin drawn as a line takes the form of a/an: (pp. 215–216)
    a. triangle.
    b. bell curse.
    c. V-shaped curve.
    d. U-shaped curve.*
    e. circle.

16. Mass communication is the exchange of information via: (p. 190)
    a. radio
    b. television
    c. newspaper
    d. mass medium
    e. all of the above.*

17. One indicator of the end of the melting pot era is the changing role of: (p. 202)
    a. assimilation
    b. acculturation
    c. demographics
    d. English language.*
    e. none of the above.

18. For many years the U.S. government, implemented immigration policies to limit the number of newcomers based on two criteria: (1) to discourage individuals with only manual work skills, and (2): (p. 203)
    a. to allow people from the professions to enter.
    b. to restrict the number of people of color.*
    c. to restrict the number of non-English speaking people.
    d. to restrict the number of elderly.
    e. all of the above.

19. A common perception is that new immigrants are poorly educated and that many go on welfare. Actually, only _____ out of one thousand new immigrants go on welfare. (p. 206)
    a. three*
    b. four
    c. five

d. six

e. ten

20. Reverse culture shock or _____ is usually a surprise to the individual, who does not expect to have adjustment problems in going home. (p. 217)

    a. sojourning.

    b. assimilation.

    c. acculturation.

    d. reacculturation.*

    e. cultural maintenance.

True/False Questions

1. The émigré cultures in the United States are unique in their behavior of adapting to their new culture in the form of a melting pot. (F, p. 189)

2. The cultural maintenance process usually occurs as an immigrant gradually learns the language of the host culture, forms friendships with a network of host nationals rather than with fellow immigrants, and becomes increasingly exposed to the mass media of the host nation. (F, p. 190)

3. One aspect of identification with an ethnic group is how others in a society perceive various individuals as members of ethnic groups. (T, p. 196)

4. The mass media have only little influence on public opinion as the freedom of speech allows individuals to inform themselves from a variety of very diverse sources. (F, p. 207)

5. Cultural bias in the media is as pervasive when it comes to gender as it is with ethnic groups. (T, p. 209)

6. The reverse culture shock is less significant as the culture the individual returns to is familiar. (F, p. 213)

7. A sojourner is an individual who visits another culture and adopts the new culture as his or her own. (F, p. 211)

8. When the media do not have a workforce that reflects the audience that they seek to serve, news coverage is unbalanced and ethnic groups in the audience tune out. (T, p. 210)

Essay Questions

1. Is the United States more a melting pot or a tossed salad? Provide evidence for your position.

2. Discuss the concepts of assimilation, acculturation, and cultural maintenance as they relate to intercultural communication.

3. What decade in United States history experienced the greatest population growth? Discuss the current ethnic demographics of the world in terms of religion, language, and geographic location. How do these compare with the corresponding demographics of the United States population?

4. Discuss intercultural communication in the media. How are non-English speakers portrayed? What kind of coverage is given to the world beyond the borders of the United States? What is the impact of this coverage?

5. What do we know about sojourners and culture shock?

6. Discuss the U-curve of culture shock and cultural reentry.

Chapter Eight: Becoming More Intercultural

Multiple Choice Questions

1. The degree to which an individual is able to exchange information effectively and appropriately with individuals who are culturally dissimilar is called: (pp. 221–222)
   a. code-switching.
   b. culture shock.
   c. intercultural communication.
   d. intercultural competence.*
   e. ethnocentrism.

2. Heterophilous contacts with culturally different people can also lead an individual to become more: (pp. 223–224)
   a. tolerant.
   b. ethnocentric.
   c. prejudiced.
   d. open.
   e. b and c.*

3. The third culture is a term applied to people who have: (pp. 223–244):
   a. parents who are immigrants.
   b. parents from two different cultures.
   c. a culture in which they grew up and another in which they sojourned.*
   d. immigrated into a different culture.
   e. all of the above.

4. In order to become more interculturally competent, many communication courses use: (p. 225)
   a. native speakers
   b. experiential training.*
   c. culture shock.
   d. training videos.
   e. empathy.

5. When we understand a culture from the inside and look at the behavior of the people from their point of view, it means that we practice: (pp. 225–226)
   a. intercultural competence.
   b. intercultural communication.
   c. cultural relativism.*
   d. ethnocentrism.
   e. code-switching.

6. The stages from ethnocentrism to ethnorelativism do NOT include: (pp. 226–227)
   a. a parochial denial of cultural difference.
   b. an offensive view of cultural difference.*
   c. an acceptance of cultural differences.
   d. adaptation of one's thinking to cultural differences.
   e. integration of cultural differences in one's worldview.

7. The origin of the word stereotype is in the field of: (pp. 227–228)
   a. cartoon syndication.*
   b. stereo broadcasting.
   c. newspaper printing.
   d. etching.
   e. early photography.

8. Which writer spoke of the pictures in our heads and the role of the mass media in forming such stereotypes: (pp. 227–228)
   a. Georg Simmel.
   b. Edward Bernays.
   c. Marshal McLuhan.
   d. Noam Chomsky.
   e. Walter Lippmann.*

9. A _____ is a classification used by individuals to categorize their experience and to communicate it to others. (pp. 228–229)
   a. sign.
   b. symbol.
   c. memory.

d. stereotype.

e. code.*

10. An unfounded attitude toward an outgroup based on a comparison with one's ingroup is called: (pp. 230–231)
    a. stereotype.
    b. trend.
    c. opinion.
    d. prejudice.*
    e. a and d.

11. In the 1940s, what did Gunnar Myrdal identify as *An American Dilemma*: (pp. 230–231)
    a. The gap between new immigrants and integrated immigrants.
    b. The racial prejudice by European Americans toward African Americans.*
    c. The stereotypes held by European Americans concerning their Native American neighbors.
    d. The lack of diverse cultures on the same continent.
    e. The prejudice of many Americans toward underdeveloped nations.

12. Which law has abolished discrimination in the U.S.: (pp. 231 & 237)
    a. no law has abolished discrimination.*
    b. 7th Amendment.
    c. discrimination is only illegal (according to federal law) in housing, hiring, schooling and other aspects of daily life.
    d. The Civil Rights Act of 1964.
    e. discrimination has been abolished in all but the Southern states.

13. The textbook gives _____ as an example of a leader overcoming prejudices. (pp. 233–236)
    a. President George Washington.
    b. President Abraham Lincoln.
    c. The Dalai Lama.

d. Mahatma Gandhi.*

e. Nelson Mandela.

14. Who experiences discrimination in today's world: (pp. 231–237)

    a. people with disabilities.

    b. people who are overweight.

    c. several religious groups.

    d. people with AIDS

    e. all of the above.*

15. Settling a conflict by facilitating understanding between the disputing parties is called: (pp. 237–238)

    a. mediation.

    b. third party intervention.

    c. neutral party intervention.

    d. negotiation.*

    e. green table discussion.

16. One of the most demanding tasks of a communicator settling a dispute is: (pp. 237–238)

    a. to facilitate when the parties belong to different cultures.*

    b. to facilitate when one party is right and the other one is wrong.

    c. to facilitate when one party has more power (financial or military) than the other.

    d. to facilitate when the parties have no diplomatic relations.

    e. all of the above.

17. What is multiculturalism: (pp. 238–239)

    a. to be able to live in different cultures.

    b. to recognize that different cultures can exist in the same environment and benefit each other.*

    c. to live in different cultures and speak different languages equally well.

    d. to recognize that different cultures cannot exist in the same environment, but must be kept separate in order to flourish.

    e. none of the above.

18. The process of finding peaceful solutions to a conflict through a neutral, third party intervention, is known as: (p. 237)
    a. negotiation.
    b. mediation.*
    c. conflict resolution.
    d. conflict solution.
    e. standardized conflict.

19. The process of treating individuals unequally on the basis of their race, gender, or other characteristics is known as: (p. 231)
    a. prejudice.
    b. stereotyping.
    c. discrimination.*
    d. ethnocentrism.
    e. ethnorelativism.

20. Direct, personal (one-on-one) contact with an unalike other can _____ ethnocentrism. (p. 224)
    a. eradicate.
    b. change.
    c. increase.
    d. decrease.*
    e. does not impact ethnocentrism.

True/False Questions:

1. Intercultural competence is the degree to which an individual is able to exchange information effectively and appropriately with individuals who are culturally similar. (F, p. 221)

2. Many tourists who visit another culture for a brief period, often without knowing the language, become more ethnocentric toward that culture. (T, p. 223)

3. The American dilemma Gunnar Myrdal wrote about 50 years ago no longer exists. (F, p. 231)

4. Mediation is more difficult than negotiation. (F, p. 237)

5. A stereotype is a special kind of code used by individuals to categorize their experience and to communicate it to others. (T, p. 228)

6. Intercultural communication training must be highly experiential in order for it to increase intercultural competence. (T, p. 225)

7. Cultural relativism is the degree to which an individual judges another culture from his or her unique perspective. (F, p. 225)

8. Stereotypes, the building blocks of prejudice, categorize others into familiar patterns. (T, p. 240)

Essay Questions.

1. Define intercultural competence and discuss its importance to intercultural communication.

2. Discuss the stages of passage from ethnocentrism to ethnorelativism.

3. What is a stereotype and how does the concept relate to intercultural communication. Give an example.

4. What are prejudice and discrimination, how do they differ, and how do they relate to intercultural communication? Include the role of Ghandi and of Martin Luther King.

5. You have been assigned to mediate a conflict between two people who work with you who are from different ethnic groups. How might you use your knowledge of intercultural communication to approach this task?

6. What is multiculturalism? Discuss its implications for intercultural communication.

Chapter Nine: The Global Village

Multiple Choice Questions

1. Which development led to the paraphrase of the world as a global village: (p. 243)
    a. the proliferation of channels for communication.
    b. the fact that transportation now links formerly remote locations.
    c. the fact that mass media now provide instant information around the globe.
    d. all of the above.*
    e. none of the above.

2. Bringing about social and economic advancement for a majority of people through gaining greater control over their environment is part of: (p. 244)
    a. global communication.
    b. global progress.
    c. development.*
    d. change.
    e. preventive diplomacy.

3. What is an innovation: (pp. 244–246)
    a. an idea that has never been thought of before.
    b. a new object (tool, machine, etc.) that performs a function different from any other existing objects.
    c. any idea perceived as new by the intended audience.*
    d. any economic, social, technological, etc., progress made for the better.
    e. none of the above.

4. A change agent is: (p. 246)
    a. a status symbol that leads to a change in an individual's socioeconomic status.
    b. a word that induces code-shifting.
    c. an action that leads to political, economic, or social change.
    d. a professional seeking to assist others to achieve a higher socioeconomic status.*
    e. a person working in a foreign stock market.

5. A change agent tries to influence and change his or her: (p. 246)
   a. owners.
   b. environment.
   c. political, economic, and social situation.
   d. customers.
   e. clients.*

6. One of the most important factors in successful development projects is: (p. 246)
   a. money.
   b. politics.
   c. sympathy.
   d. synergy.
   e. empathy.*

7. _____ is the degree to which a development project continues to be effective after the original development effort ends. (p. 249)
   a. success rate.
   b. sustainability.*
   c. endurance.
   d. empowerment.
   e. none of the above.

8. The dialogue of women dairy farmers and their trainer given in the textbook is an example of: (pp. 249–250)
   a. emancipation.
   b. endurance.
   c. empowerment.*
   d. sustainability.
   e. empathy.

9. Which institution came to be seen as a magic multiplier in the 1970s: (pp. 253–254)
   a. United States Government
   b. television.
   c. World Bank.
   d. radio.
   e. mass media.*

10. Ethical issues play a role in development projects: (p. 255)
    a. because the goal is to convince other countries of the idea of progress and not to persuade them.
    b. because of the increasing number of relationships between the people who are being helped and the helpers.
    c. because the harmful consequences of the development project sometimes outweigh the benefits.*
    d. because of the strict N regulations for project personnel.
    e. because the lack of intervention has sometimes caused major catastrophes.

11. The recent growth of cities has had an enormous impact on which one of the following forms of communication: (pp. 256–257)
    a. interpersonal.
    b. intrapersonal.
    c. mass.
    d. intercultural.*
    e. social.

12. Which cities will experience the largest amount of population growth: (pp. 256–257)
    a. cities in the industrialized countries in the Western Hemisphere.
    b. cities in Asia.
    c. cities in Africa.
    d. a and b.
    e. b and c.*

13. _____ is also known as the United States capital of the developing world. (pp. 256–257)
    a. Miami
    b. New York City
    c. Los Angeles.*
    d. Washington, D.C.
    e. Chicago

14. Which company recalled its product after several Arabic nations threatened a boycott for something so obviously making fun of their religion: (pp. 256–257)
    a. Anheuser-Busch (Budweiser beer).

b. Victoria's Secret (women's lingerie).

c. Levis (jeans).

d. Nike (sports shoes).*

e. Hefner Corporation (*Playboy* magazine).

15. Which scholar stated that the superficial shared experience implies the world's movement toward a global culture: (p. 263)

a. Edward T. Hall.

b. Robert Park.

c. Georg Simmel.

d. Marshall McLuhan.*

e. Thomas Steinfatt

16. The exchange of information between two or more individuals in which one individual seeks to assist the other individual to achieve a higher socioeconomic status by changing his/her behavior is: (p. 244)

a. development.

b. development communication.*

c. development programs.

d. sustainability development.

e. empowerment.

17. In the next few years, _____ will surpass Tokyo as the world's largest city. (p. 256)

a. Jakarta.

b. Bangkok.

c. New York.

d. London.

e. Mexico City.*

18. Intercultural communication between the poor and the rich involves differences in _____ as well as differences in meanings. (p. 256)

a. knowledge.

b. language.

c. resources.

d. power.*

e. stereotypes.

19. The degree to which learners become aware of their oppression and are motivated to change their underdog situation is: (p. 250)
    a. development.
    b. development communication.
    c. consciousness-raising.*
    d. empowerment.
    e. client heterophily.

20. Companies today must design products to fit diverse cultures, advertise them in numerous languages, and meet the demands of different consumers. This is known as conducting business in: (p. 258)
    a. megacities.
    b. mass media development.
    c. development programs.
    d. global advertising.
    e. global marketplaces.*

True/False Questions

1. Most change agents try to understand their audience's point of view. (F, p. 246)

2. A key ingredient in sustainability is the communication relationship between the development project leaders and the people the project is intended to help. (T, p. 249)

3. As a result of industrialization and modernization, Japan also became completely Westernized. (F, p. 259)

4. Developing nations see themselves as victims of a one-way flow of communication. (T, p. 263)

5. The authors' goal in writing their book was to provide skills to break through the cultural boundaries separating us from others. (T, p. 264)

6. The empowerment criterion of development interventions meant that programs had to be carried out with the conscious participation of the intended audience. (T, p. 250)

7. Although the change agent may be heterophilous, opinion leaders are homophilious with others in the system. (T, p. 248)

8. The effects of the global village—an increasingly smaller world of tomorrow—can be reversed. (F, p. 243)

Essay Questions

1. What is development communication? Discuss its importance.

2. How does the concept of heterophily affect change agent interactions with clients?

3. Why should we be concerned with the sustainability of development programs, and what do we know about sustainability?

4. What is empowerment? Discuss its effects on intercultural communication.

5. Why did Nelida's efforts to introduce water boiling fail? What intercultural communication lessons can we learn from this failure?

6. When is it acceptable to introduce a change into someone else's culture? State as clearly as you can an ethical principle you would be willing to apply throughout the world for determining when such interventions are justified.